The Gulf Stream Poems of the Gulf Coast

Art by Katie Lukas

Jeff Newberry and Brent House
Editors

Snake~Nation~Press

Valdosta, Georgia

Published by Snake Nation Press
Valdosta, Georgia 31601

Printed and bound in the United States of America.

Copyright © Authors 2013

All Rights Reserved

No part of this book may be reproduced in any form, except for the quotation of brief passages, or for non-profit educational use, without prior written permission from the copyright holders.

ISBN: 978-0-9883029-4-5

Cover Art by
Heather Newberry
and
Katie Lukas

110 West Force Street, Valdosta, Georgia 31601
www.snakenationpress.org

Saint Island Prayer

Align us, o beauteous earth
with your purposes.
Open our ears, our inner and outer eyes
to the particular work you would have us do
to the work we fit as closely
as the plunging tern, embraced by salt shallows
as the palm deeply rooted in shell mound
as the wind, wrestling through it all
and beyond, the glaring sun.

We are hungry to know what we may do.
We listen and watch
We attend.
Our lives are so short, our hearts, so strong.
We know that in serving your life forms,
We also serve ourselves.

Teach us to be
as persuasive as the pelican
as inevitable as the ancestor
as peaceful as the oyster
as relentless as the raptor
as relaxed as the tide
as reliable as the moon
as present as the palm to the wind.

Susan Cerulean
Indian Pass, St. Vincent's Island, Florida
November 2004

CONTENTS

Susan Cerulean	*Saint Island Prayer*	3
Introduction		9
About the Editors		13
Dedication		14
Bruce Alford	*Econarrative*	16
	Spill	17
Roebud Ben-Oni	*Econarrative*	19
	Returning to Sal Si Puedes	20
Miriam Bird Greenberg	*Econarrative*	23
	I Passed Three Girls Killing a Goat	24
	It's Hard to Forget	25
	Seasons Changing	26
Ash Bowen	*Econarrative*	27
	Letter from a Mistress	28
	Yearbook Photo of My Parents, 1959	29
Bredt Bredthauer	*Econarrative*	30
	Reverend Haggard's House of Pleasure	31
	Silence	32
Adam Clay	*Econarrative*	33
	Extinction Rates	34
Brittany Connolly	*Econarrative*	35
	Holiday, 1929	36
Peter Cooley	*Econarrative*	37
	From the Gulf	38
	Locales	39
	Meditation at Crescent Beach	40
Daniel Corrie	*Econarrative*	42
	Of Being and Becoming	43
Meri Culp	*Econarrative*	47
	Venus Flytrap, Green Swamp	48
Gwendolyn Edward	*Econarrative*	49
	Corpus Christi	50
	Leaving the Coast	51
Ann Fisher-Wirth	*Econarrative*	52
	BP	53
Brett Foster	*Econarrative*	57
	Recovery, Gulf Coast	58
	Various Pairs of Twins	59
Rebecca Morgan Frank	*Econarrative*	62
	Blue Mussel Shells	63
	Crawfish Chorus	64
	Postscript from Mississippi	65

J. Bruce Fuller	*Econarrative*	66
	Boy, Age 9	67
	On Seeing the Ocean, from 35,000 Feet	68
Natalie Giarratano	*Econarrative*	69
	Low-Water Mark	70
Joshua Gottlieb-Miller	*Econarrative*	75
	Forces of Spiritual Danger in.....	76
Jeff Grieneisen	*Econarrative*	77
	Scorpion of the Woodpile	78
	The Birds Repeated Warnings	79
Glenn Halak	*Econarrative*	81
	1946, South Florida	82
	Bahia Hondo State Park	83
Carolyn Hembree	*Econarrative*	84
	[O pony of South Derbigny o leaping yellow]	85
	Fox Ode	87
Katherine Hoerth	*Econarrative*	89
	The Bull Rider	90
	"Adan y Eva" in the Rio Grande Garden....	91
Thomas Alan Holmes	*Econarrative*	92
	Gulf Shores, 1968	93
	Pascagoula	94
Alice Johnson	*Econarrative*	95
	Before Hurricanes Had Names	96
	Gras Doux	97
Julie Kane	*Econarrative*	98
	Purple Martin Suite	99
	Womanish Blues	101
	Birch Thoughts in Louisiana	102
Greg Koehler	*Econarrative*	103
	Alabama River Dirge	104
	Atchafalaya River Dirge	105
	Mississippi River Dirge	106
John Lambremont, Sr.	*Econarrative*	107
	The Wood Grows Silent	108
Chip Livingston	*Econarrative*	110
	Burn	111
	Defuniak Springs	113
Cleopatra Mathis	*Econarrative*	114
	The Faithful	115
	On a Shared Birthday: J.C.L. 1953-1979	117
	Salt Water Ducks	119

Karla Linn Merrifield	*Econarrative*	120
	1564: The Virgin One	121
	The ABCs of Everglade Hurricanes	122
	Learning the Tide Tables of Grief	123
Benjamin Morris	*Econarrative*	124
	Highway 49 (to Gulfport)	125
	Highway 26 (to Wiggins)	126
Brent Newsom	*Econarrative*	127
	Smyrna	128
	Esther Dreams of Floyd for the Third....	129
Deborah Paredez	*Econarrative*	131
	The Gulf, 1987	132
	Elergy for Donald Clark, Assistant Driller....	133
	Corpus Christi	134
Alison Pelegrin	*Econarrative*	135
	Pantoum of the Endless Hurricane Debris	136
	Hurricane Party	137
	Ode to the Pelican	139
Bin Ramke	*Econarrative*	140
	Resonance	141
	Among the Functions of Flowers	142
	Aleatory Agilities	143
Martha Reed	*Econarrative*	145
	Land and water (1)	146
	lapse :: a city	149
Billy Reynolds	*Econarrative*	151
	Huntsville Stars	152
jo reyes-boitel	*Econarrative*	153
	Chan Chan	154
	footnote to the romantic life	155
Katherine Riegel	*Econarrative*	156
	And That Life	157
	Acridophobia (Fear of Grasshoppers)	158
	We are Gulls	159
Rena Rossner	*Econarrative*	160
	Aubaude with Citris	161
Mary Jane Ryals	*Econarrative*	162
	After a Funeral at Cedar Key, Florida	163
	Winter Beach Sighting	164
	What ocean does	165
Danielle Sellers	*Econarrative*	166
	Friendship Bracelet	167

	If I Died Now,	169
	December Evening, Key West	170
Matha Serpas	Econarrative	171
	Betsy	172
	Conversion	174
	The Water	175
Paul Siegell	Econarrative	177
	*05.04.07 - New Orleans Jazz Vipers.....	178
	*05.05.07 - Jonathan Freilich, Skerik,.....	179
ire'ne lara silva	Econarrative	181
	tierra	182
	diabeticepidemic	183
Jay Snodgrass	Econarrative	186
	Apalachicola	187
Andrea Spofford	Econarrative	188
	(Oncorhynchus mykiss)	189
	Victoria, Texas	190
Sheryl St Germain	Econarrative	191
	Lake Pontchartrain	192
	Crossing the Atchafalaya	193
Sunnylyn Thibodeaux	Econarrative	195
	Evangeline, How Do You Call Your Tribe	196
	Not Quite Colorado Bound	197
Jay Udall	Econarrative	198
	Louisana 1 South in Winter	199
	To An Armardillo	200
Jerry Wemple	Econarrative	201
	Half a Mile Off Everglades City, Florida	202
Patti White	Econarrative	204
	Sarasota	205
	Bovine	206
	The Air in August	207
Anne Whitehouse	Econarrative	208
	Blessing III	209
	Blessing XXXVI	210
	Desecration	211
Harold Whit Williams	Econarrative	212
	Still Life with Methodist Youth Retreat....	213
	Yonder Cries the Gull	214
	Bones in the Bathwater	215
Contributors' Notes		216
Acknowledgements		227

An Introduction to
The Gulf Stream: Poets of the Gulf Coast

What I stand for is what I stand on.
— Wendell Berry

With the landfall of Hurricane Katrina in 2005 and the subsequent failure of the levies in New Orleans and with the explosion of the BP Deepwater Horizon oil rig in the spring of 2010, the Gulf Coast region of the United States has been thrust into the national spotlight. No longer just a region, the Gulf Coast became a political hotbed, a fulcrum in an ongoing national dialogue about the federal government's responsibilities to its citizens, and a pawn in the debate over domestic oil drilling and government regulation of the oil industry. And while these issues are central to many Gulf Coast writers, the Gulf Coast is more than a political touchstone. The purpose of this anthology is not to address Hurricane Katrina or Deepwater Horizon. Instead, our purpose is to capture in print a swath of poems shaped by the poet's relationship with the coastal landscape.

The term "Gulf Stream" refers to a warm current of water that shapes the development of the weather and tidal patterns that define the Gulf Coast. The Gulf Stream affects nearly every facet of life in the region, from the weather that even those inland must endure to the waters fished in the Gulf of Mexico. Appropriately, this anthology borrows the term to refer to those poets whose work has been influenced or shaped by their relationship to one of the Gulf Coast states: Alabama, Florida, Louisiana, Mississippi, and Texas. We've also included some poets from South Georgia, a region that's culturally and geographically very close to the Gulf of Mexico. These poets represent a cross-section of poetic aesthetics: from mainstream and otherstream, from personal lyrics to experimental meditations. What binds these poets is their connection to their landscape. They are all a part of what we're calling the Gulf Stream.

These poems capture an endangered way of life. The growing global climate change crisis virtually guarantees that the Gulf Coast region will radically change in the next fifty years. This anthology, *The Gulf Stream: Poems of the Gulf Coast*, seeks to capture the tensions in this American borderland through the voices of poets who can enhance our understanding of the ecological, historical, and cultural forces that have shaped the region. These poems are the voices of a Gulf Coast that future generations will not know.

Because catastrophic global climate change has forced the culture of the Gulf Coast to reevaluate its relationship to the land, the poems in this anthology reflect a concern with the natural environment. Not "eco-poetry" per se, these poems nonetheless explore the complex interrelationship between those who call the Gulf Coast home and the land itself, the natural environments that provide for and sustain its residents. The poets in this book have been witness to the changing environments on the Gulf Coast. The wide and diverse experiences explored herein underscore the unifying aspect of the landscape. These poets may all emerge from different socio-economic backgrounds and different aesthetics, but their works all reflect the importance of the landscape and the Gulf of Mexico. This anthology brings together both native and non-native poets of the Gulf Coast, all who understand the central place of the natural environment in the region.

This anthology argues that how one speaks about the land affects how one thinks about the land. And how one thinks about the land necessarily affects how one treats the land. The poems in this anthology are far from mere "nature poems" that eloquently describe the environment (though certainly, many do just that). Rather, the different modes of poetry within these pages work to "tear" a reader awake, to paraphrase Forrest Gander, viscerally jerking a reader into awareness of the Gulf Coast. What these poems share in common is an interest in a natural, actual landscape (and, by extension, the psychic landscape developed by that region). In focusing their attention on the real, verifiable world, these poems argue for the importance of the natural world. The diversity of the poems presented herein only further underscores this importance. Poets from vastly different schools of thought are united in their concern with the region.

As such, regional literature plays an integral role in shaping the way that cultures think about and act toward their landscapes. To some, "regionalism" suggests a provincial literature unconcerned with larger, universal questions. This anthology argues that regional literature can become a lens through which we view those things that unite us: regional concern like catastrophic climate change are, after all, global concerns, as well. The editors of this anthology call for a new regionalism, a literature of the land that is less concerned with local color and urgently interested in the preservation of the natural environment. To be clear, this new regionalism is not some Agrarian call for the good old days. Rather, a New Regionalism insists on radically different ways of thinking about how the literature of the environment represents and responds to the natural world.

The editors of this anthology believe that a New Regionalism has already begun to awaken in the United States. Consider the rising popularity of local farmer's markets, the whole foods movement, the rising popularity of roots/Americana music, and the growing weariness with irony and self-reference. This New Regionalism isn't anti-human, as some extreme environmental movements have been. Humans occupy a central space on this planet. We have the capacity for advanced thought. We have the ingenuity and the brilliance to build and to exceed our species' capabilities. As such, we have a profound responsibility to take care of the land, even if we don't believe in any higher power. Humans are central on planet Earth, and with that central position comes much, much responsibility, which we've ignored over the years. We can quibble and argue about the existence of God and the origin of life on Earth. We've done so for over twenty centuries. We cannot, however, argue about the ground beneath our feet. It's there. And when we ignore it, it changes, for the worse.

The editors make no claims to the religion of any of the writers included in this book. But both editors believe that a right understanding of humankind's place in the natural environments is deeply spiritual. From a Christian perspective, God in Genesis placed Adam and Eve in the Garden of Eden with explicit instructions to steward the land. We believe that humans have been poor stewards of the natural environment. It's time that we take responsibility for our actions. If we are to preserve and secure our home for future generations, it's time that we become better stewards.

As Susan Cerulean, Janisse Ray, and A. James Wophart write in the introduction to their anthology *UnspOILed: Writers Speak for Florida's Coast*:

> We believe in the power of our artists and writers and naturalists to help guide us in this time when desperation and greed have come disguised as virtues. Our story is deeply intertwined with the story of this place . . . that we all—Democrat and Republican, liberal and conservative—have worked so diligently to protect. To speak for [the land] is an act of faith, a belief that hope will prevail over desperation, that good sense will triumph over greed.

Like Cerulean, Ray, and Wophart, we believe in the power of the spoken word. The editors don't advocate parochialism. Right stewardship doesn't emerge from some misguided sense of superiority. We care about the land because we care about ourselves and we care about future generations. Caring for and preserving our natural environments is simply the right thing to do.

Each of the following poems is preceded by an "eco-narrative" (a term suggested by Heidi Lynn Staples). This eco-narrative grounds the writer's work in the Gulf Coast region, explicitly connecting poetic inspiration with the landscape and seascape. We chose to place the eco-narrative before the poems to emphasize the poet's connection to the region. The poets are listed alphabetically, preferring no one Gulf Coast region over another.

We offer these poems in praise of the Gulf Coast where we are grounded. To be grounded is to be aware of the shared world. To be grounded is to have one foot on the ground, another foot in the water, and to feel that reality.

—Jeff Newberry and Brent House, August 2013

About the Editors

Brent House

Brent House, author of *The Saw Year Prophecies* (Slash Pine Press) and contributing editor for *The Tusculum Review*, is a native of Hancock County, Mississippi, where he raised cattle and watermelons on the loamy soils of his family's farm. His poetry has appeared in journals such as *Colorado Review, Cream City Review, Denver Quarterly, The Journal,* and *Third Coast.* He serves as an assistant professor of creative writing for California University of Pennsylvania.

Jeff Newberry

A native of Florida's Gulf Coast, Jeff Newberry is the author of *Brackish* (Aldrich Press) and the chapbook *A Visible Sign,* a nominee for the Conference on Christianity and Literature's Book of the Year. His writing has appeared in a variety of print and online journals, including *Apalachee Review, Barn Owl Review, The Chattahoochee Review, storySouth, and Waccamaw: A Journal of Contemporary Literature.* He's won scholarships from both The Sewanee Writers Conference and the West Chester University Conference on Form and Narrative. His website is http://www.jeffnewberry.com

To Bunyon and Colea and the soils they farmed.

Brent House

To Heather and Ben and the rest of the crew.

Jeff Newberry

Bruce Alford

In grade school, I learned French, and every year my elementary school principal would read to us the Christmas story of Papa Noel, the Cajun Santa who was led by alligators instead of reindeer. As a kid, I picked strawberries at many of the Italian-owned farms and when the harvest was over, we'd celebrate with a *Cochon de Lait* (a Cajun pig roast). We'd dance to Cajun music and eat cracklings cooked in a giant skillet.

My upbringing reveals the Gulf Coast's rich cultural heritage. I grew up in a small, segregated African-American neighborhood called "Grace Quarters," probably named for one of two Henry Grays who lived in the early 20th century, either Henry S. Gray or Henry T. Gray. Both men derived their livelihood from working wood. One was a logger, the other a carpenter. This region of the Gulf Coastal Plain, the northern upland region, is replete with pine and water. Here is where my best friend, Twain, and I built a raft and went poling it through a canal; we ended up being chased by dozens and dozens of snakes waking from winter hibernation. This is where a white kid who lived next to a dump taught me how to catch snakes and then how to make belts from their skins, and this is where we hunted squirrels and rabbits, ran after good "coon" dogs and where we caught baby alligators.

Water was everywhere. Grace Quarters was surrounded by canals and ditches—a good thing too—because this region, like Mobile, Alabama where I currently live, is known for its floods, hurricanes and tornadoes. Fortunately, the beaches, warm winters and Mardi Gras, the South's great pre-lent celebration, more than make up for the occasional hurly-burly.

Spill

It is Sunday morning on the Mississippi.
Oil has washed up on the bank.
Absorbent booms soak it up.

A barge loaded
with blue steel containers
appears to spread

across the river, that rippled skin
of brown.

Oil in water
Smooth oiled stones tinted rust
or tire black.

Large chunks of metal have shivered
and now, the whole thing resembles some
surrealistic, aleatoric sculpture garden.

Young black men like Rayvon Carter
pick up oil-soaked mops with pitchforks.

Rayvon wears
the side of a pasteboard box on his head —
protection from the sun.

Bare Cypress gnarled and filigree of roots,
mooring lines washed up on shore:

everything is always
wet

inside the levee.
An old man leans against a 74 Ford
parked on top.
You can still see the boy in his face.

His log-shaped arms
seem made of oxen-white hair.
He wears hunting fatigues.
And that block in the pocket,
that's a pack of Winston's.

He squints at the sky,

against belief and insects,
and lights a cigarette.

At least the oil will kill the insects —

among them worms
sheathed
in a warm laziness.

Rosebud Ben-Oni

My mother is Mexican, and my father is Jewish; a large part of my childhood was spent with my mother's family on the Gulf Coast near Matamoros and Brownsville, as well as the Rio Grande Valley. My grandfather holds a lasting influence on my work. A fisherman by trade, he taught me how to swim so that I knew what it felt to have nothing solid beneath me. At the time I was four years old, and small for my age; the breakers easily knocked me back to shore. My grandfather was swimming a few feet in front of me and insisted that I had to get past the breakers to get to the calmer part. He told me to dive into the waves just as they were building. I remember thinking: you want me to dive into what is knocking me down? But eventually I did it and found another world entire. His fear and respect of the ocean made quite an impression on me.

I also inherited his love of parrots, especially the wild amazons that cross back and forth over the border. He would find those wounded or sick, and nurse them back to health in large, wire cages he kept outside his house. (And that house—how I loved that house—three rooms that once contained nine people: my mother, her siblings and her parents.) After my grandmother died, my mother and I would stay the night, and I remember waking up and running outside to see wild amazons kissing the caged amazons through the wires. It made me upset for some reason, and I'd start howling and chasing them away, and my grandfather, usually such a solemn, serious man, would start cracking up as he made us breakfast.

Returning to Sal Si Puedes

> —Sal Si Puedes means "leave if you can" and is the name
> for many a town; this one is on the U.S.-Mexican border.

In summer I return from where
I was sent away. I loiter around *we*
in which they gather, seek the familiar

italicized in old school books,
made foreign by teachers.
Salsa. Tejano. Margarita.

Back then Texas Rangers shot up the windows:
You a Marine, ese? And detention
for speaking Spanish in the hallway.

Fifteen minutes away from the border
and mostly Mexican,
home was fading "Anglo Town."

My mother was Class Favorite,
but the newspapers refused to run
her picture crowned Queen Cardinal

because her name was Esperanza Gomez.
She insists I wear my sandals inside,
frowns when I drink from the faucet,

for wanting to savor the same bitterness,
bottom-speckled, as if I've never known
anything but this.

Over on the island, tap water
bleaches the fish
even in quick rinses.

Fifty years ago the shorefront was sold
for next-to-nothing,
but we didn't have that, they remind me.

MTV has made South Padre into Matamoros,
and Matamoros is now shuttered *maquilas*,
bad soil and *sicarios*-in-training.

I drag out the old vacuum,
as amazons on open t-stands
'cock an eye and flatten to unease.

Go ahead, they sing from the kitchen,
rewashing dishes I already did.
Don't you remember?

I flip the rusty switch
and jet-black sounds fill the room.
I drop the hose in fear

while they puff up and dance.
I forgot the disturbance
reminds them of hurricanes,

that love bare-footed
and beyond censor.

The joy of entering into the fray.

I jerk across the cracks,
and drone into the noise
that it hurts when you wash your hands

before touching my face,
kill the chickens while I sleep.
Tell me again why the leaves of palms

double as branches,
why crossing the desert
wove wolves into our steps.

Once I too swam the canal,
ran long, mountainous distances
for which we were made.
I go too far and nearly pull

the loose socket from the wall.
The amazons fall back

into spitting feather and seed.
Someone settles my hands,
tells me not to trouble:

Always the room returns
to how they want it,
to we in which they gather.

Miriam Bird Greenberg

Over the past few years, I've focused on refining a manuscript of poems that form the loosely interlocking narrative of a woman fleeing unnamed civil upheaval a hundred years hence, partially set in the rural dystopian future of the Texas/Louisiana Gulf Coast and the East Texas Piney Woods. A historically diverse and lawless region, in the past the Piney Woods was a place where freed and escaped slaves made their lives, American Indians migrated to avoid white settlers, lawbreakers hid from the law, and many others thrived. This manuscript follows the narrator as she finds herself, as in Alice Notley's *The Descent of Alette*, in negotiations with the travelers and ghosts who people this landscape of fluid borders and national identities, where the boundaries between the known world and another are permeable. In my work I'm interested in exploring rural dystopias, reviving folktales and legends traditionally associated with early America, recast in the light of a post-Fukushima, post-Katrina & BP world. I grew up in northeast Texas not far from the Piney Woods (near Paris, which is strictly speaking blackland prairie—a totally different feel), in a ramshackle house built by my ancestors when they first settled in Texas a hundred and fifty years before. Through my childhood, owls dragged their claws across the attic floor every night, two hives of bees lived between the first and second story (on hot summers honey would drip through the ceiling into the library), and for a while my favorite hiding place was the fallen-in blacksmithing shed behind the house, near the limestone path where the National Road ran during the Republic of Texas. As I came of age as a writer, the geographic and cultural histories I'd grown up amid became more and more central to my work; the ghosts of my ancestors populated the margins of poems, and though the 'plot' of each poem is a confabulation, the landscapes surrounding them are often autobiographical. Having grown up on a working farm in Lamar County, a childhood spent working with animals and exploring my family's fast-decaying property has bound me to the land, its history, and to rural living—even as I make my life happily in cities far away now.

I Passed Three Girls Killing A Goat

I passed three girls killing a goat, shotgun
leaned up against a tree and the entrails
spilling into a coil on the ground. It was hooked
between the tendons of its back legs
to a high branch that gently creaked
like a dry hinge busybody aunties wouldn't oil.
Blood drained into a pail, you could smell it
shifting with the air, and black flies landed
in the shadows of things where the wind
didn't touch. I dreamed I was carrying a sack
filled with animals, and it dragged blood
in the gravel and stained my skirt hem, you could follow
my trail to the county line where old men
sat on the liquor store porch. One crooked his half-arm
for the bottle where the auger had caught his hand.
I dreamed I was in a new country rinsing livers
under a spigot, and the men cracking
black walnuts on a stone named my limbs
like the weather, like none of us knew
the same words. By the tree the girls and the goat
were faltering, one squatted to sharpen
her blackened blade on a strop, and the men
on the county line leaned back on the heels
of their chairs talking about anything, each other,
spring weather, the long-haired boy scalped
by a combine, and one of them swore you only plant
beans with the moon in Capricorn otherwise
the fields choke up with scrub juniper. One
looked intently at his left palm; his right wrist
uselessly brushed the woven seat of his chair.
When a wind came, the screen door leapt up
on its leather hinges which never creaked
and slammed shut. Mud daubers in the muck
by the spigot blew sideways around my ankles
and inside I could hear the woman
who lived with the liquor store proprietor
cursing as she locked up the vanilla like she knew
how to break the back of a ghost.

It's Hard To Forget

It's hard to forget what I ate when the waters receded:

certain earths, ashes, limestone, cornstalks. Frayed fabric
picked faintly away as if by mice. June bugs. Mice. I craved
friable china clay

from a vein in the pond's berm—ate that, and took duck eggs
to sell in town, though more and more the ducks bore pale
shell-less eggs encased in translucent membrane; those
I tore open, cooked outdoors
in a bone-handled coffee can. Disaster's stratum

marked the abandoned kitchen's clapboard walls and slat-backed
chairs: where flooding
had paused for a moment (as if waiting in an orderly way
water has never once done) then moved on. Hemline ravel threaded
to a fine thorn,

I gathered false mending, stitched gold filigree
beneath the fabric folds of a jacket in case one day
it came to me to leave

suddenly. Already half the county had scattered—gullies
gathered left-behind bedrolls, the debris
of mementos too heavy to carry
 flecking the fields—but thieves had emptied every barn
of its turning forks and hay-hooks, heavier still. Inside mine,
the sun canted

against an aging ox-drawn plough, daybreak sundial
for wanderers to this place inhabited by wreckage,
the packed-dirt floor
specked with bones. Untouched by turmoil,

a pistol lay dissected on the workbench, its interior coils
unsprung, musculature retained in its minute landscape even still.

Seasons Changing

In the long spring falling out of love was a task I set myself to,
and I found preoccupation with frogs diving into gullies,
the truckers idling all night in gravel parking lots
of sagging restaurants by the highway.
Voices from the road played off as spirits asking who
      left the ringing phone unanswered? Who
           left the laundry blown into trees untouched?
On the edges of towns: lonesome greyhound track, miles
of furrows,
the roads ploughed narrower and narrower every season, now a
single dirt path
winding through the fields.

Dark on the creek bed the cranes fly low and lean, wings heavy
against the body of the heat. Snakes shed their skin long ago, lie
coiled in the damp of outhouse soil and find in their languor a task
to set themselves to.

The pecans drop their branches in wind, loosen pollen in tassels.
Slowly the barns cave in,
trees felled by lightning give in to decay, the broken crockery
doesn't mend itself, the fields set afire by the falling sun blaze

unextinguished night after night. We begin to ask
the unanswerable questions. Who
      turned their shoulders to the wall at night
when owls shrieked in the grape arbor? When
      ghosts of women scuff their feet on the floor upstairs
and light reflects in the eyes of every dead thing, why
      would you leave the door unlatched? Hair clippings
in the waste basket?

The husk of a body left
asleep under low light, the story unresolved: who left
the milk to curdle, let the eggs roll sideways off the counter?
The fields burning all autumn are a want larger
than any lover can assuage.

Ash Bowen

Pat Conroy wrote in his novel *The Prince of Tides*, "My wound is my geography." In many respects, I feel a kinship with that statement. When I think on my time in Louisiana, I recall the pregnancy and birth of my son—a joyous occasion to be sure—that just so happened to coincide with my first marriage becoming an instrument of torture for all parties involved. And later, in Texas, I found my second long-term relationship eating itself from inside—a process that took years to complete.

All of this is to say that my poems are born out of those pains and locations. As a poet, I find myself constantly returning to Texas and Louisiana to try to make sense of the emotional violence that occurred there. Like many Southerners, the specter of religiosity is ever-constant in both my life and my writing, and though it may only be obvious to me, many times the poems are attempts to seek atonement for my sins.

Of course, I'm not writing autobiography. Poetry is not nonfiction, as Miller Williams has said. But the language of autobiography is constantly peeking out from behind the curtain at almost every turn, and standing in the back, always watching, are Louisiana and Texas waiting to see how they show up in the poem.

Letter from a Mistress

I was a bird when you wanted a wife.
So I flew, collecting what I knew of wives —
hotel keys to unlock
the lace they lay across their down-
less bodies, champagne
corks to keep their mouths
from buzzing all the flowers.

You made me a hummingbird. Blur
of desire. One word, sir. Finish
what you started. Here is where
you hung your promises. Hear them
hiss across my body.

Yearbook Photo of My Parents, 1959

In the picture, Mother's not my mother yet.
Lithe and barely 20, she leans into the frame

of the sorority kissing booth, eager
to meet his lips.

He's counted out his love, professed it
dime by dime.

They've kissed like this for 60 years
inside the camera-snap,

their ardor unchanged by time.
But the camera's caught more than that:

my father's restraint.
Barely there in the flash

of history, his face inches
forward from the photo's lower corner, watching

the footballer whose kiss shuts my mother's eyes
like rapture.

In the picture, it's nearly 1960.
My parents' faces young, unworried

with the future. Soon they'd graduate
to a life they never imagined, not knowing

how often this kiss would be remembered
every time my father wanted to fight.

Bredt Bredthauer

I was born in Houston, Texas and grew up in the humidity of the Gulf Coast. As the son of a construction worker and a substitute art teacher, I never got to travel very far for holidays. Every year my family drove southward and stayed in a variety of seedy motels from Port Aransas to the South Padre Island area. Don't get me wrong; the smell of rotten fish and saltwater still makes me a bit nostalgic and reminds me of home. After attending college in Texas and working in a variety of jobs, I moved to Florida where the Gulf Coast was once again just a short distance away. For three years I spent a significant amount of time traveling to Cedar Key and many points south to kayak and explore the coastal area.

The most interesting experience I have had along the Gulf Coast, however, involves a long bicycle tour from Austin, Texas to St Augustine, Florida. Needless to say that traveling along the coast on a bicycle laden with panniers at no more than ten miles an hour was amazing. I learned more about the people, culture and geography of the Gulf Coast in that period of time than I ever expected. People invited me into their homes in cities everywhere from Bay City to New Orleans to Naples. Although I continued riding my bike to New York City and then overseas from London to Sicily, the Gulf Coast remains one of the most hospitable and interesting places I've found.

Reverend Haggard's House of Pleasure

I find comfort at the stripper bar in Panama City.
Destiny brings me another shot of Patrón tequila
while, on stage, Venus bares her nipple rings.

Because the eye awakens the body's desire,
I hand Candy fifty dollars for a lap dance
while Prince sings "Purple Rain."

No one bothers to ask me about my day
or how to eliminate the passive voice
from a narrative poem.

I should drive home, buy milk, mow the lawn,
and make lesson plans for class tomorrow;
yet nights like this remind me of my father,

how he spent days on end watching strippers
spread-eagled on stage while ordering
Reverend Haggard's House special—

a pint of Choc Beer and twenty-five-cent wings.
I abstain from saying words like *mother, daughter,*
and *son*, because it takes a forgetful mind to enter

this building. At nine o'clock sharp, Venus climbs
a metal pole, and strobe lights break across her body.
The face of Minnie Mouse is tattooed on her back.

Men in seersucker suits stuff bills
down her red sequined thong as she extends her legs
far above her head, like the points of a cross.

nce

Compelled by the smell of salt cod,
I sit down beside my father as he coughs
yellow phlegm on the floor and flicks
ashes across the Formica table.

My mother is cleaning Corning dishes.
Her fingers look like fish, her hair like ink.
I listen to her ragged breathing and stare out
the window where a river rises and recedes.

Foolish as it sounds, I find solace
in watching water move away
from the walls of this double-wide trailer
and, in our driveway, the archaic El Camino

that bears a black bumper sticker proclaiming:
God Bless Ronald Reagan. A Playboy calendar
celebrates the upcoming millennium.
We watch fog crawl across the dark

surface of the river. Our roots
extend beyond this world to another
where the mind submits to nothing.
It slowly annihilates our names.

like a still life

Adam Clay

For me, the Gulf of Mexico has always been a metaphor for the imagination. I was born in Hattiesburg, a short drive from the Gulf, and I always found something so calming about living close to the coastline. Perhaps it's the idea of another life happening close by, another type of life mirroring our own. When the oil spill happened in 2010, I was in Mississippi visiting my family, and on April 22, Earth Day, my wife and I celebrated our fourth anniversary in the terrible uncertainty of the Gulf. Who would have known that oil would spill out until July? My relationship to the natural world has always been an important one, but after the birth of our daughter, the connection became even stronger. In writing "Extinction Rates," I wanted to somehow eulogize the Gulf of Mexico, but in writing the poem, I realized how futile this act could be. If the natural world is a mirror of our own existence (and I hope it is), it seemed to me that if I were to eulogize the ocean, I would have to eulogize human nature as well. I live in Kentucky now—twelve or so hours from the water—but I still feel a closeness to it, one that persists throughout my imagination and in my poems.

Extinction Rates

An investment gone wrong
doesn't easily forgive the one

who invested. What strange
space a field can occupy

if one's concept of a level field
comes straight from a textbook

or word-of-mouth. I had been
trying to describe a fish

to my daughter, one
that I caught in a stream surely

dried up by then.
A bee had been moving

across the top of the water —
and then I remembered

she had never heard of a bee so I tried
to describe a bee, though this

was much more difficult,
aside from the fact that we were

running out of time. I'm not
sure I have the right to elegize

an ocean, but it's clear that more
could fit into this strange portfolio

than I had first imagined, a fact
dull among a thousand others,

a fact not nearly worth
repeating or celebrating.

Brittany Connolly

I grew up in Fort Lauderdale, Florida, which is opposite the Gulf Coast, but my fondest Florida memories were in Naples, just across the state, where my family vacationed frequently. It was close enough to get to without too much time in a cram-packed car, yet far enough away to notice a real difference in the Florida beaches. I remember sinking my skinny fingers down into the soft, pearly sand to dig up the most vibrant, multi-hued clams I had ever seen, and when I'd free them from my grasp, they'd bury themselves deep in the wet sand just below the surface. Between the spectrum of colored clams and the turquoise surf, it was my favorite place to be as a child. It was this that I'd look forward to every time we got a chance to get away for a few days.

I find that the Gulf Coast region commonly pops up in my writing, both poetry and fiction, because it was a vital part of my upbringing. One of my poems, "Something about Settling," focuses on feelings that manifested themselves after my short visit to the coast of Louisiana, and it's one of my favorite pieces to date because it brings back rich reminiscences.

I still yearn for that return to my second home, the home I loved most, back on the Gulf Coast. Now that I live in Tennessee, as an adult, I am finding ways to get back to my roots. I decided to attend graduate school in Tampa, Florida, so I could smell that salty Gulf air again, and I assume that Florida will reclaim me one day, as it should. Between the Gulf Coast, the Everglades, and, now, Appalachia, I find my culture to be a rich and ever-evolving aspect that informs some of my best work as a writer.

Holiday, 1929

Twenty nine and fine in dime store blues, rich-
At-heart. Organdy girls in silk-collared Basque dresses
Meet men in three-piece suits. Maiden skins, pale like almond milk
Pretty in the moon, 'til the Tampa sun bakes them bronze.
And how lace-laden ladies love those silver minarets! — stretching ears at

Belfries to listen for the hurried rings of silent, hollow spires.
Anxious men bear tear-burdened eyes, spying on unfaithful wives —
Young lovers sheathed in bed sheets on California Kings that

Haven't felt such an urgent heat since summer, 1923.
On and on those jazzy vinyls spin like dainty dolly carousels,
The sizzling Fats Waller ditties fill the lobby with crack-n-pop notes of
Ebony and ivory plunky keys. When it stops, guests stand still
Like marble effigies, only blushing back to life during a holiday refrain.

Peter Cooley

The Gulf of Mexico and The Gulf Coast region, where I have lived over half my life, have come to be a part of my way of seeing, all the more, perhaps, because I lived the first half of my life so far inland — in Michigan, Illinois, Iowa.

My first visit to Sarasota, Florida, where I now own a condo, made me aware of The Gulf of Mexico as a constant, a daily mirror where I could examine myself. It is impossible to leave our place in Florida without confronting that mirror. At night I can hear it breaking up, preparing me for another day when I can be reflected in it. And reflect on it.

Most of my poems explore internality. But that inner world can only be shown through its reflection in the kind of water and sky the open worlds of the Gulf Coast and the Gulf of Mexico make possible. They make possible the grounding of my speaker. I am enclosing three poems which partake of that grounding.

From The Gulf

High summer the clouds here are motionless,
they have nothing to do with us
the lives we chose. Over the water
they roll back mornings tapering
at their ends, flecked like eggs
a giant sea bird warmed and fled.

And the palms, how quietly they bend
their shafts through white heat, trembling
the upper branches, quivers
in the noon's calm. How strange
at the beach each one of us appears
naked to ourselves and yet a body

Greek deities took on in stone.
While from the surface of the ocean,
at evening, shaking off the foam,
the fixed stars' stare has risen
with their reflections, found their name:
light, light and nothing we can be.

Locales

After the last gulls, the scavengers
for Florida shells, the couples leaning
years on each other, after teenagers
leaving the beach the angles of their thighs,
the shark boat shrilling its all clear finally,
the clouds turned, sterns to leeward
across the gulf, a trawl of white fire
stretching to Texas.
                    And there they stood,
two boys straddled by two girls
sexless before adolescence, fully clothed
in black, disguised all afternoon
as shadows on the whitecaps, shallows
of their robes like priests', the full skirts,
long sleeves, swollen, dark with water.
And then they turned, themselves again,
children of the Mennonites, washing me up
on sand still warm before the clouds
lifted, put out to Mexico.

itation at Crescent Beach

1. The First Prayer

This is where I find myself:
in the eye of the pelican fixed
on nothing, the sky taking his wings,
describing wide arcs, gliding down
over the dark water, hovering.

Or here: where old men come
to squat, high tide around their necks
beside their wives and silent, motionless,
take the undertow, righting themselves.
Steadier, the women draw them in.

And here: the shore beneath my step
 releasing the sea into itself.
This is the middle of my life,
I stand at the edge of it, waiting.
Over the low tide evening will come down.

And now: I whisper to him
Soul, fly out of me till morning,
leave my body darkening this water,
then turning home, darkening his bed.
Take me with this word. And I open my lips.

2. The Ecstasy

Quiet of six o'clock in the morning.
Over the gulf's still water
light hovers, shapes itself
to these first birds.
                    Now it rises,
circles wider, gilting pines,
the white sand beach under my feet.
Then, crossing dunes, I'm calling him,
wading shallows with this darkness
I've carried here: soul, soul,
take the form of gull or tern

or pelican—spirit, come down,
let the deep give you my name, surrounding it...

And if you answer, all day sun
will follow me, until I reemerge
through bodies, corridors, the kind of night
no bird ever sees. And if you don't,
later I'm back: ant, mosquito, mite, sand tick—
one of them will take you before dark.

3. The Leavetaking

When I am done with this life
I will come down here
at nightfall, while the tides go out
and they will not return alone.

The rocks will be slippery, black.
Around my ankles will be rainbows
washed up with oil, I will be watched
by fish in it that never stir

except to be cast, washed out,
cast, headless under my feet.
I will stand very still and wait.
The wind will bring everything to me:

voices huddling windows at my back
light up the dark; the scent of pines
sways like a censer; now the mourning dove
keeps a choir on the air, invisible.

I stand here, facing the sea
where it stretches up, touching the sky
and the sky falls quickly to meet it.
I fasten myself to that thin line.

And give my name up, give my face
to the emptiness and hear it answer—
voice, come into the darkness—
and the water is cool about my feet.

Daniel Corrie

In the six years since moving from Atlanta to South Georgia to settle on my wife's family farm, my wife and I have worked at eco restoration, including thinning 80 acres of densely planted "tree crop" slash pines to be more hospitable for wildlife, which remarkably increased the presence of gopher tortoises, a keystone species. Burning off these acres resulted in a resurgence of long-dormant wiregrass and other native understory. Additionally, we planted 60 acres of longleaf pine and native understory. Soon after settling on the farm, my wife and I became reluctant activists, devoting a year to fighting full-time in partnership with several groups to oppose a coal-fired power plant planned for a nearby county, which our groups' efforts defeated. My wife and I have been active in the local food movement in rural South Georgia, including working in partnership with friends in organizing well-attended conferences promoting locally, sustainably grown food. Art itself might be an act of ecological restoration. Do I believe poetry can make a difference? Yes, I do—or I wouldn't write it. Given the severe human impact on our planet's biosphere, Joanna Macy has called ours the time of the Great Turning, when our species is turning to fundamentally new ways of thinking and doing. Thomas Berry wrote of what he called the Great Work, when people from all walks of life, including the arts, might turn their energies and gifts to finding our collective way into what Berry called the Ecozoic Age.

Of Being and Becoming

> ~ I am divided up in time, whose order I do not know.
> —St. Augustine

Its insect mouth half formed, never to feed,
one mayfly will be born in spring
from the cool creek

to find the feel
of its veined transparency of wings
beating to climb,

needing what was never taught,
joining the sexual cloud
of its swarming kind.

Each will roughly clasp or be clasped,

their flurry hurrying
to clasp their winged lifetime's
single day.

Sometimes from fathoms of sleep,
I rise swimming
from my forgetting

ancestral fins, scales, gills,
feeling water turn to wind, pulling me
from the swarming plankton's
wide, bluegreen womb of water.

Now water narrows, birth canal
through forest into clearing.

From the field's gleaming
seam of creek, I walk
in my scuffed boots and mud-spattered jeans,

feeling sweat soak the back
of my neck's binocular strap.
Sweat gives me salt's taste

of something almost as lost
as dimmest memory of tasting
breath in sun-dimming depths.

Fifty years have been
too sudden for knowing
where I've emerged walking,
looking, listening — then to hear

the scream, again and again,
to look up to the high hawk's
broad wings cocked,

riding the rise of morning's
warming air, higher with each circle.

It screams its hunter's ownership
of the territory beneath
its called claims.

This March's hunter
will die to a future's twin hunter
climbing other mornings' circles,

screaming the same scream.

In one of the dreams,
a god stood, totem unchanging,
shape risen to a pillar,
perfection's looming monolith

beyond years' rains melting
temples' ruined, toppled columns.

I've seen a column rise into sky,
column of a forest's smoke.
Each tree was fire's pillar.

Smoke's column soon drifts, form hazing
as if forgetting itself,

as a dark sky will clear
to stars, like leaves' cooling embers
drifting through a night's air.

A creek's course will dry to earth-scar,
left like a memory of water running.
Each of my creeds fell like sunlight
in a creek's water braiding

sometime through time's
long season of making,
unmaking, making.

Again blind rain will need
the arid creek bed to flood

re-carving its shape,
ancient shape
of skin-changing snake —

shape writhing in its shedding.

Time: transfiguring
triptych of past, present, and future —
Great swarm of triunes

of beginnings, middles, and endings —
I stand in the memory of water rushing
one morning through sunlight,

lost creek unlost
where I crossed, stopping ankle deep,
kept in its going — keeping its going,

where I was — where I am.

Great form
of transformation—

Enduring shape
of metamorphosis—

Sometimes I hear the parable
of my past reciting me
like a future.

Sun-filled in my seeing,
creek's current was a clarity
like the good. Its vein of feeling
might course as clearly

through a life's blood-blush—

through blood's reddening horizons

of duskdawn into duskdawn
of now into now.

Meri Culp

For me, the coastal area of the South is defined by both the water and the land: the history both hold, the rhythms of the currents and sifted soil, the overlapping of waves and shore. It is a place of both slowed down time yet sudden movement, natural world surprises.

Flytrap, Green Swamp

The venus flytrap is not all about death and sex and pink entrapment,
the Eve-lure of entering, of woman-fear red, *opening, closing,* sins

of ruby-throated hummingbirds, nectared up, hovering over, dipping into
leafed pleasure, shadowed dewdrops, russet underbrush,

but instead, the venus flytrap, freed from mythology, her temptress ways,
rejects the spellbound eyes of humans, their fly-feeding pleasure, their need

for green, for teeth to clamp, hard, to open to pink, smooth, strangling;
over and over they watch, but not today,

not in this green swamp, not in this hidden dampness where
connotations wash away: *sacred,* the blue Carolina sky; *profane,* earth's nature,

finding the voice of Venus, not trapped, feeding, food-chained
to all things simple, : *opening, closing,* small winged sounds, the sift of reeds,

spined survival, the zig, the zag, alligator shift, green-mouthed,
lily-pad mute, then blooming, floating by Venus, unfettered, native, tongued.

Gwendolyn Edward

When the Deepwater Horizon oil spill occurred in 2010, like many others, I was horrified to realize the extent to which our daily lives threaten the natural environment. When I went to the Gulf Coast in the summer of 2012 with my boyfriend's family for vacation, I went expecting to see no remnants of this disaster, and I didn't. But what I did see was equally disturbing. In Port Aransas, hotels along the beach have tar showers. There were goblets of black, waxy substance both in the water and along the beach. At night, I could see the blinking lights of at least three refineries in the distance, and I knew that the ecological threat was not something that happened only when there was what we'd call a disaster; it was all the time. I was further unnerved by the lack of conversation of those around me regarding this issue. Even worse, I saw children picking up the tar balls and playing with them.

That we take our environments for granted is upsetting to me. That on a daily basis, we're contributing to the tangible decay of our planet for the sake of convenience leads me to think about decay in all of its forms. After the vacation, I began to write more poetry about the deterioration of the self and how our actions (and inactions) regarding the Gulf Coast are reflected in the aspects of our daily lives: we're detached, unwilling or incapable of reconciling our actions with the environment, and it will require a great deal of introspection to arrive at conclusions about our responsibilities.

Corpus Christi

My boyfriend's father struggled through the sand
to the cabana, a foot long shark, black finned,

in his hands, the wicked hook still through its cheek.
Children squealed and with greed, touched its skin

while he peeled the hook out of its face, gently. But
he had a length of thin rope and he fashioned it

into a semi-noose, slipping it over the head
of the shark. Then he walked the creature

in the surf, on a leash. I could see the taut string
and the white foam, the globs of tar on the sand.

My eyes stung with too much salt and I closed them.
That night, the shark, admired too long in the sun,

drowned in the water. It washed up on the shore and
opened its mouth twice. Only a small spotted crab

witnessed its death, then retreated to the hole it had made
only minutes before. The crab returned with others,

and began to eat it. Began the process of returning.
My boyfriend and I had sex on the balcony above and

after, we spoke of adopting a child. But the conversation
sounded somewhat like waves and I could not listen.

Leaving the Coast

The wind brings the smell of diesel and not the smell
of salt, anymore. My forehead is pressed against the window
and it is hotter where the sunlight makes bars
on my arm. I've left the ocean brown and scarred

thinking of all the tar on the beach, and in my lungs.
Texas is flat and whoever said the world is round
has not been here. It looks like a savannah, and I do not see
elephants or gazelle, though they live in parks nearby,

"Animal World" and "Snake Farm." I remember once, driving from
Dallas to Jackson, the gas station along I-10 that advertised
a lion. There was a jar on the counter with a thin strip of paper
that read: "Please donate so our lion can have a pool."

Outside it was humid and there was a concrete enclosure.
Children without shoes and a man with baby powder on his hands
stood near the fence like it was Coney Island, while the lion
hid in the shadow of an artificial rock, his mouth gaping open,

mane matted, eyes not even full of curiosity, or hunger.
I did not give money to the lion so he could have his pool.
I bought a lemonade that I used only as an ashtray so the grasslands
would not burn to the ground. We both did not trust men

working at gas stations. I drive and see a tree leaning and flat.
A canopy that belongs. It is a thing of the desert and in its branches
is a shining, blue foil heart balloon. It is caught, still,
still full of helium, and looks out of place, but appears perfect.

Ann Fisher-Wirth

I teach English and direct the Environmental Studies minor at the University of Mississippi. Many of my students come from the Gulf. Many of my students' family homes were damaged or destroyed by Hurricane Katrina. One girl told me about a spindly purple chair that had come down from her great-grandmother through the generations, that she was inch by inch restoring; it was the only piece of furniture she could rescue from the flood. One guy, an M.A. candidate who had gone down to teach high school in New Orleans, accidentally left his laptop and thesis when the call came to evacuate, but saved every one of his Bob Dylan CDs.

I am writing this three days after Hurricane Sandy ravaged the East Coast, seven years after Hurricane Katrina should have been a wakeup call. I am writing this in an electoral season in which global warming, climate change, global climate disruption have not been mentioned specifically by either presidential candidate. In terms of compassion and speed, President Obama's response has been everything that President Bush's was not. In terms of preserving the chances for life as we know it, little is being done despite these cataclysmic warnings.

Then there's BP. And two and a half years later, Romney's promise that if he wins he'll instantly grant permission for the XL pipeline and for drilling in the Arctic, and kick it into high gear for oil, gas, and coal.

We are all shaped by the Gulf. The problem is, we refuse to know it.

BP

1.

Serious harm or damage to life	**Dear Sirs:**
(including fish and other	
aquatic life), to property,	**Dragonflies**
to any mineral deposits (in areas	**hover**
leased or	**catching the light**
	emerald, turquoise, ruby, translucent
not leased), to the national security	
	Born of water
or defense	**they sport with land**
	but lay their eggs in water
or to the marine, coastal, or human environments;	
	where oil clogs the membrane
blowouts, fires, spillages, or	**of their**
other major accidents. . .	**wings**
	Above the slick among the grasses
	one dragonfly scrubs
	its oiled face
a threat of harm	

or damage to life. . .

filthy

iridescence

to take affirmative action to abate

the violation

2.

The pelicans spread their feathers

spiky and stiff with gunk

Now that we are beyond the oil-covered-

birds phase, establishing definitive

links between the spill and whatever

biogenetic

or ecological disturbances are in store is

strain forward above the slick but   only going to get harder.
. . .

cannot rise

Graveyards of recently deceased coral,

gape, flap   oiled crab larvae, evidence of bizarre

squeak and bark, squawk

flail   sickness in the phytoplankton and bacterial

communities, and a mysterious brown

amid sea oats

viscous water

                liquid coating large swaths of the ocean

        floor, snuffing out life underneath. . . .

                consequences as severe as

      commercial

Contaminated

    inside and out

the pelicans mottled

    with poison

                fishery collapses, and even species

                      extinction—

3.

"I have not been there, I have not seen it.

It means little to me, a matter of blogs and soundbytes.

Not ordering oysters at the oyster bar."

Flames roll over the waters,

lick the legs of our chairs

where we sit sipping coffee.

Quoted phrases in Part 1 are from the National Commission on the BP Deepwater Horizon Oil Spill and Offshore Drilling January 2011

Report to the President.
Quoted phrases in Part 2 are from Naomi Klein, "After the Spill," *The Nation,* January 31, 2011.
The italicized lines at the end of the poem are from our anonymous, collective response.

Brett Foster

Instead of longstanding, or even native, experiences in Gulf-Coast states, my poems were inspired by my own different kinds of encounters with the Gulf Coast— those encounters than seem all the more profound, and can make the one experiencing them all the more impressionable, for being entirely new. Or if not new, exactly, at least a needed, deeply needed break from daily life and a more quotidian landscape.

"Recovery, Gulf Coast" reflects the many visits I have made to visit in-laws and family of my own in Texas. These visits have primarily been to Corpus Christi, and my wife's mother and step-father are fortunate to live just a few blocks from the Gulf Coast shoreline, on Paloma Street, whose name has always entranced me. The sonnet in its different ways tries to dramatize how these visits for me enact needed oppositions or alternatives— sickness to health, cold to warmth, stress to rest, the daily to holiday, and, in the final image, something like the shift form work, left behind up north, to something like pure grace and beauty, as symbolized by the young neighbor girls at the poem's end.

"Various Pairs of Twins" owes its inspiration to the Florida landscape and locale. I have even less of a claim to being a Florida writer, but sometimes the places that most dazzle us and illuminate our writing are those places that, once we finally arrive there, feel like a great discovery of the senses, of capacities for perception itself. That's how it was for me when I was able, at long last, to visit the Florida Keys. The first Florida poem's structure is based on itinerary, but quickly shifts into an "itinerant" mode that celebrates the freedom and caprice and openness of the traveler. In the poem's drama, peace is sought at the edge of the world. The second poem is a more free-wheeling, cavalier engagement with a particular place, and the community there whose local color matches the colorful surroundings well.

Recovery, Gulf Coast

– at Christmastide

Visiting in-laws outside Corpus Christi,
I feel whole again, healthy in swell weather,
silent in this deck chair near the mesquite.
Chicago and the snow seem far from here,
my hacking cough that fogged the windshield.
Calm prevails like sailboats off the balmy bay.
Not this place only, but because the everyday
recedes against the yard's edge. Then the children!
They play behind me, where it laps the curb.
Buoyant in their running bodies, our two squeal
in sweaty chorus with the neighbor kids,
who all have lovely names: Celeste, Camille,
Chloe. Three graces: zealous, undisturbed.
Or heavenly virtues: trio fresh from hiding.

Various Pairs of Twins

Land of broken bridges, or necklace
of islands, and today I'm wandering
roughly around the middle of this place,
mid-afternoon, stopping abruptly at this branch
of the Monroe County Library
forgotten and sun-beaten here in the Keys,
cooling my face with the cooler's ice,
the rest of me with a holy margarita
got from a taqueria across the street.

Approaching the door and the cool air
behind it, I pause to take a few more
sips before tossing the plastic cup
in the handy trash can— *keep Florida*
beaches clean! on the upturned lid.
Just a slice of shadow noticeable,
and curbside's fairly quiet. I'm preoccupied
with taking in my surroundings.
In the adjacent lot there's a sheriff's
substation, which an abler reporter
might call similarly "hardscrabble."
And on the building's modest back patio,
a palm-lined space lined with pavers,
a jump-suited inmate deftly directs
a line of spray from his garden hose
across the rows of tiles, covering
the entire square footage. He does it
with style, spinning his wrist and angling
the spigot here and there. His upbeat
demeanor seems, improbably, in touch
with the fluorescent orange color beaming
from his uniform, state's property.

Rude of me, probably, but I'm really
honing in on him as I finish my drink.
His instinct is to finish with one last,
grand wash-off, and so he stakes himself

in the farthest corner, taking position.
Working in stillness now, he sweeps
his hose from left to right repeatedly,
left hand placed conveniently on his hip.
That's when I notice the both of us,
our spliced postures fifty yards apart
from each other, but otherwise there
to witness our separated circumstances
briefly being reintegrated, together again.
I too am standing with my hand on my hip,
so that we make for each other a perfect mirror,
that fellow middle-aged white guy,
brown-hair prisoner of fortune, earning
his bed, biding his time in a different way.
Of course we say nothing to each other,
but then again the view that we share
speaks for itself. Each sizes up the other,
and smiles, even, as if we were both
saying, "Well there you are, finally."
For one minute there's nothing at all
impaired between us, no despair
hovering over us, darkening this sun-lit
harmony and concord, like a grand piano
whose cover has been folded over
for the youthful impresario, full of energy,
just undertaking his world tour.
I feel an urge to say, "I miss you" —
what am I saying? So turn away.

But first I think of that woman, a twin.
She's thirty years old in nearby Waukegan
back home. Her sister, the one
who babysat on that fateful day
nineteen years ago, was murdered.
"I have never been known for myself,"
she said through her heroin addiction,
but always as the dead girl's sister.
Lately she wears her name like a label
on her neck — *My missing half*

in ink on her skin, announcing its gravity
with elaborate loops and serifs,
further engraved with wings and halo.
"How would it have been if she were here?"

Untethered now, released
from my bright doppelganger
across the way, I suddenly
notice the others around me:
a beach-combed woman
walking out of the library,
walking and talking baby-talk
to her groomed Pomeranian,
and a biker dude and chick
clad in dark brown leather,
covered in sundry tattoos,
clicking away on the bench
aligning with the sidewalk,
tapping away on two laptops,
one lit up and beeping in each lap.
Far be it from me, I determine
solemnly, to harsh their mellow,
a phrase I handily picked up
from a lesbian in a Key West club.

Rebecca Morgan Frank

To move to Southern Mississippi post-Katrina and post BP's oil spill in 2010 is to face a landscape whose physical and cultural nature are changed in concert, at the hands of both humans and natural forces. The attempted separation of human and ecological concerns falls apart in a place where poverty prevents surface cover-ups of the effects of disasters on the inhabitants of this beautiful and battered region: I continue to be startled by both the destruction and the strange beauty to be found here. The sunrises intensify and the struggles of those watching do to. Do I sound like an observer? I still am, as a new inhabitant who may live out her life in this new place. These poems reflect the beginning of my struggle to begin to see what's around me, to hear it. As a poet, I'm often first drawn to the ugliness, such as the adapted features of alligators and crawfish, unfamiliar bodies even to someone from Virginia. And of course the ugliest view is the poverty I see: here our country's history and weaknesses simmer at the surface of things. Poems are a way for me to try to understand how celebrating this place is to name its wounds and to find how the need for social justice is bound in the landscape, from the water to the people who live on and from it.

Blue Mussel Shells

Ripe wrack and ruin, that's not a life.
The strife of a swallow, black-
shelled along the bottom. Sand me
down to the grit shawl, wait.
I can open. I can stretch my jaw
like an alligator and move
the whole town through this
swamp. Easy. I was born below
these trees. I saw the birds seed
and die, the water move through
like a train. The highway melted
around and made new moss.
I waited and waited for the rounds,
the swing up. But that's for
the bees. They never once
get swept out to the Sargasso Sea.

Crawfish Chorus

Crawfish, crawfish, Mary caught a dogfish. Dog face, dog race, send her down Brown's place. One, two, three, the roof's done broke free: now the water comes down and lifts us up. You are not it. And the wind whirls round and lifts us up. And the wind rolls round and puts us down. Lightening strikes twice. When the morning light levels, synthetic gauze holds sky back from sea. Sea back from land. Land back from river. If you reach right in, a catfish. If you reach right in a catfish. Will swallow your arm and spit you back out. You swallow it. Chase it down with a coupla crawfish. Craw. Craw. Craw fish. Crawling. Fish.

Postscript from Mississippi

When you asked if it rained bees or poison
you were asking the wrong question. Again.

You still didn't understand the difference
between hurricanes and flooding. Thus between

gods and humans, I said. Between your
slum-lorded digs and the shack I pass that clings

to the old boards and huddles around
a family. Matched by its neighbors.

Everywhere something is falling on
someone and I watch like an autumn

tourist tripping through the Berkshires.
I reach to catch a leaf. I try to straighten

a Pisa-like sapling. The wind wraps around
us both like a question mark and leaves

me standing, the sole witness on this end.
I'm telling you about a place of silence.

You want it all to be a metaphor. I'm watching
a front porch crumble. Still, someone sits there.

J. Bruce Fuller

Someone once asked why I wrote so much about water. I didn't understand the question.

Eventually I answered that in my entire life I had never lived more than four minutes from a body of water. I grew up around the woods and canals and bayous of Louisiana. I could drive a boat before I could ride a bicycle. The rivers and lakes, floods and hurricanes, have shaped my experience.

Woods and water are almost characters in my poems. I think this is because both can act for the good or ill of those surrounded by them. This is not nature "red in tooth and claw" exactly, but neither is it an idyllic sanctuary. Water can kill you here, in more ways than one. The woods can harbor or harm. We are surrounded by a landscape of decay and death, but also of an abundance of life. This dichotomy is a part of my mythos.

Perhaps that is a better answer to the question, perhaps not. My grandmother used to say that we don't pray for rain, because you might get what you asked for. She was right, of course.

Boy, Age 9

This is what I learned of dismemberment.
Hunting squirrels with my uncle,
I learned to track them through the trees,
to walk beneath their rustle and chase.
When the squirrels noticed us they froze
and lay flat against the mottled bark.
It was my job to walk noticeably
across the straw covered ground
and move them around to expose
the squirrel's splayed back to him.
The scattershot would hardly ever kill them,
but drop them like a top to the wooded floor.
I learned to grab them by the tail
and flail them fast against the trunk.
I learned to listen for the moment of death,
that hollow crack of skull on tree
like acorns falling on a tin roof, early winter.

for Bhanu Kapil

On Seeing the Ocean, from 35,000 Feet

This could be *our* water,
all the rivers and streams
and bayous of home,
where we will all end up
in the green-blue wash and churn.
The ocean is black now
after nightfall, and from this height
it could be asphalt, or mud.
But some sense of it is there
to swallow us if we fall.

I am on my way to the old country
my forefathers left,
but I am thinking of my father,
who is watching my children
play by the waters
of the brown Beouf River.

I ask him through the glass
if we are happiest at such distances,
or if sons and fathers are bound
by the waters that surround them,
and he answers with a wave
that stirs the darkened clouds
beneath the wings.

Natalie Giarratano

Everything is brown. The soot from refineries coats the grass, the buildings, buries itself in our nostrils, lungs. Working class until there is no work, then move or work hard somewhere else while children miss their fathers or until the body breaks down.

Our Gulf is a muddy brown in which I've never wanted to swim. Never step in to dance with the jellyfish that look dead but are still alive enough to sting. To pray with their bellies up toward the sun.

Everything is brown in my town, except for the people, who can shine like the specks of jellyfish on the Gulf sand of my mind. People I admired (and in some ways still do) until I left my small southeast Texas town and found out how insular, how guarded my family (huge Catholic family) was and is and that the roots of that guardedness have grown in the darkness of sexism and racism— some women afraid to drive at night or to be home alone while their husbands work graveyard shifts, some men in my Sicilian family with dark skin and hair who look down on others with even darker skin, some men and women who will never reach their full potential because of all of this fear. This isn't necessarily indicative of the South or the Gulf region or small town sensibility. But since the landscape of my childhood embodies all of these things, this landscape that also finds a home in my poems becomes complex and unique but also representative of issues that still persist in our larger society.

Low-Water Mark

1
Sometimes I can't help but walk through
a parking lot of snow without feeling
in my feet, but I don't think about
the numbness there in the middle of the lot

when the crunch of the day-old slush
makes a lot more sense than an old song
that serves as the backdrop to something new.
(There's a thousand you's and only

one of me's), and our landscapes run together
on good days before the worry
of stock numbers or being only
one of a hundred colors in a box,

and billboards talk to me, say *"Auf Wiedersehen,"*
but I'm not sure what I'm saying goodbye to;
I'm not sure what I've seen that makes it time
to feel nothing beginning with my toes

and ending, just ending.

2
Texas, Summer, '84:
no clothes required,
definitely no shoes.
That's how we roll
out here in the boonies.

Soon, some mom
will make us put on underwear
(at least), but no one
ever notices us girls
slipping on

wet trampolines or running
through movie frames
the way thin city kids run
through a hydrant's blast.

These bodies opened up
to sky were once
flares for regret;
but are we, scratched
out of water, still
the dangerous ones?

3 *London*
Before I was born,
Jack wrote: *The sea
does not know you,*

and I believed him
for a while because
I'd never even seen

the sea, nor could I recall
the slosh of the womb
from which I was cut.

But when I was old enough,
he showed me the man
who could sing through trumpet,
Davis
and from then on I knew that,
when Miles turned his back
to me, he'd thrust my soul

through that brass;
and, eventually, the sea

would have to know me.

4
There is no sea. Not in the way
it's usually meant. Some say:
metaphor for memory.
Movement of the past

in the belly of it all,
those other versions
of us wanting to be
recognized, even if blue-

green haze distorts,
makes bodies (words)
look prettier than if
witnessed first-hand again.

I'll live with this no-sea,
just thirsty sand to tiptoe across.
I'm no graceful girl, though,
and jellyfish everywhere.

5
If you turn off that sound,
green bodies of the frogs
that stick to your bedroom window
will no longer watch over you;

you, a girl who plays the part
of some button from
a moth-eaten coat that no one
hands over to the junkman.

(You can't turn off that sound.)

Crickets keep you up for the rest
of your life or at least until you claim
that shaking heart in the wake of a 3 a.m.
train that's so close to your window

you forget again your little fist
was ever there pounding to
the locomotive rhythm, so close

you could sing it to sleep.

6
Several times I've read
that one day
this place
will only be memory,
but what else
would sisters want
if not to remember
anything that could save us.

Lured to the empty
space and the poem
writing itself, I begin to
wonder if memories
are evidence of someone else's
wanderings, and if the blue
robe of this land is
the coal that the whole
neighborhood's
been choking on since
before I was born.

7
Sea shows up on our bodies
like bruises from fists
that hit
all by themselves.

It appears too quickly
to hold in meaning.

Not all girls know how
a good fight should be played out:
when the past contracts,

expand. When it expands,
adapt like a shadow to
a madman who goes all out,
scratching, grabbing, kicking,
and so on.

This kind of fight wasn't
passed on by Christ trying to
save us from ourselves;
his was for the rush of the fact
that he knew he could've
changed the outcome
had his miracles not been
consumed
by bread, fish, and water.

8
The Gulf of Mexico will not turn me
the brown of my grandmother's roux.

I've tried to scrub the naked off,
but skin has a funny way
of anointing itself.

And still I wade here
while missing persons
dislodge from the reefs

with rusted out buses
that keep shifting
in pursuit of those mouths.

Joshua Gottlieb-Miller

I spent the first few years of my adult life in Houston, in many ways a great town for an artist: cosmopolitan, cheap, and home to some of the most interesting museums in the country. I was lucky enough to live by a park with a running trail and a Japanese garden, my neighborhood was filled with the most fantastic live oaks, and it was rare for me to feel completely isolated from nature. Over the course of a few years, those snatches of green kept me from total urban bewilderment.

None of that satisfied like a day hiking or wandering the beach, but when I traveled outside the city it was rarely to the forest tracts or hill country further inland. Galveston was my most frequent respite, its beaches looking out on the Gulf of Mexico. I know I'm not alone in my love for the small seeming infinities of nature, the way the water seemed so much bigger than the land I was standing on, a feeling the Gulf never failed to deliver. At the same time, Galveston offered its share of reflective irony: a town centering its growth on tourism, increasingly at the whim of changing weather systems and dangerous exploratory drilling.

From the beach I could see oil rigs out in the open water, but I would rarely spend any time looking at them; the water seemed vast, and full of enough horizon to ignore the occasional blight. This sense of fullness and possibility was true on sunny days, during unrelenting rain, even when it was still dark at four in the morning. The Gulf was not just mysterious, but darkly transparent.

Forces of Spiritual Danger in Dangerously Spiritual Places

Maybe it was mystical to sober up on that jetty, fearing rest is reckless
as the water comes in black and silky blue, when the sun looms

above full-dark clouds. Lightning so close we cannot hear the thunder.
Only close behind us. Don't mention the girl in the hospital still.

Don't mention the bird, more blue in the sky, the holiness we didn't
add to rocks and dirt, the sand, the winds like steel cables strung loose,

fallen around a swinging bridge, and the coast completely sober, even able to drive
as sleep went back the last town over. My heart's in the right place

but my mind's gone. Don't visit the girl in the ICU. She doesn't want to see us
look at her. The hospital skeptical of inner liberty if we require it.

The beach letting the last dark stars sober in the night. Let's focus
on the sunrise we can't see: the clouds a blue flame on low oxygen—

yes, we are alone. Sad lasting remnant of a birthday party, but not even
really sad, and not even really alone, waiting to see what we are seeing

as it changes right before our eyes. Prayers only meant to be heard.
Unwanted desires. Don't tell
anyone what you can't survive. There is no escape from the escape.

Jeff Grieneisen

To me, writing about the gulf coast of Florida is always about trying to reconcile myself with this unfamiliar landscape. I grew up in the mountains of western Pennsylvania, and those mountains will always be my home. In writing about Florida, I feel that I must evoke the process of reconciliation in others, as so many Floridians are really people from elsewhere. Some exoticize the landscape; others demonize it. I see a little of both. Here, dirt is sand and the critters that evolve without regard to hibernation seem a little more primal, the foliage more tenacious. After a couple of years, I was finally able to write about this place—Florida—with some finesse, and many of these Florida poems are included in a prominent section of my first book, *Good Sumacs*.

No matter which landscape, northern or southern, my writing tends to feature the interactions and struggles between people and their environment. On the gulf coast of Florida, this interaction includes the economic drive to develop land even though that development destroys the beauty of glades and swampland. Everything evolves, and in evolving, struggles. In my writing, I love to explore this struggle for survival and speculate on the meaning of such interactions. Many aspects of the gulf region will certainly continue to evolve: the political implications of drilling, the delicate balance of human development in natural environs, these all create a kind of struggle that must be examined. And that is the role of the poet: to examine this balance and make some sense of it all.

Scorpion of the Woodpile

I stood against
the armored crab of the woodpile,
an enemy I didn't know in Pennsylvania. Here
I watch him wave the venom sword
over his dry, crisp body like a samurai.
At first I can't tell where his face begins.
I don't know if I even need the log
against this slight chill in Florida.
But the samurai must have eggs
here, or a family, or just a place
to wait for the dew that collects
in secret spaces between the logs.

He doesn't move when my chin touches
the log he's on.
After a stillness, he seems to crouch,
holding his stinger ready.
His translucent body betrays
veins that run claw to brain,
down the back and into the tail.
Some local kids know how to slice
the tail, hold it with outstretched arms,
and chase girls to show they're tough.
The scorpion will not die after using his stinger
like the bee that left its tiny heart pumping
venom through my finger when I was young.

I do not crush him as I should.
This one will live long enough to be eaten
by one of the half dozen species of bird
that picks lizards from the palmettos.
I will gingerly move the logs aside
without reaching into dark crevices,
without disturbing the almost invisible warrior
who crackles, dry, in secret spaces
wishing only to be left alone.

The Birds Repeated Warnings

The birds repeated warnings
in the shrill voices of lost children.
I sat by the pool, listening to cockroaches
crying like crickets against November.
How do we mark the passing of time
if not one cigarette butt after another?

In a corner of the living room
lies a space where the old vet's hospital bed
used to sit, a frightening hand-crank model
perched like a wounded heron,
its leg stuck straight out as if it survived
some strange accident.

I gather up the butts I used
to count the day's descent
so I can go in, pause
before the empty space.
Maybe I'll pray
for the first time in a long time

and I'll plan to visit the cemetery,
to scratch out a space
with a trowel so anyone can plant
peonies, chrysanthemums, or violets.
All the while, starlings repeat
the warning cries of fallen soldiers.
They seem to call me from my planting.
I follow their warnings to the tree line
beside the cemetery, where they fade
like black snow into the twilight of the woods.

I wonder if I'll ever make it to the cemetery,
if I'll ever scrape away that clay and mud
so that anyone can fill the space with color.
It's been a long time already, and I'm still sitting
in the front yard next to the sumac
where dark birds peck seeds
from the red clusters of soft berries.

Tomorrow I will go. Yes, tomorrow
I must go so the space in the living room
can be used for something else.
Until then, I must count days
and listen to the warnings of birds
who know better than I do
how to make the day end.

Glenn Halak

Two forces at work: the memory of a soft, humid teeming beauty and the visible consolidation of technologies, both virtual and physical, encrusting over the skin, human skin, animal skin, plant skin, planet skin, so that all that seems to remain is reason as a globally politicizing weapon of salvation, aka the fear of death and its immense shadow of greed engendering more and more death. If the blind go stumbling around telling everyone how things should look and in their wake so much is dying, what can be done to cure them of blindness? Does human existence pivot on how many want to hear only gentle lies and happy thoughts so they can go on doing what they are doing? It's the doing to things that's the essential devastation, the attempt to be in control denying softness and teeming and beauty. Can people be taught to love? These forces, the beautiful and the toxic, have always seemed so dramatically present in my early childhood memories from Florida and Texas, and then later as I re-experienced the region, the toxic began to far overshadow the beautiful. Nothing particular regional about that but the memories of the beauty I knew as a child turns all too quickly to sadness.

1946, South Florida

In oleander gardens long ago a woman with a cane,
a small boy dressed in white,
beyond the beach the dolphins whistled at the sun,
Atlantic waves wore white as well.

In mangrove roots a turtle's slimy shell,
black spiders lined up on an emerald leaf,
a man was swimming out to sea,
his clothes abandoned in the surf.

In oleander gardens long ago a mother and a child,
a dark blue rain on dark blue sea,
an empty beach for miles,
the tide was going out.

What's left when grief is all you have?
Pale fish, and crabs in piles, the smell
of swamp at night, of senseless fingers,
endless cars, their windows stained with light.

In oleander gardens long ago a morning moon
was hiding in the trees, soft as kisses on a cheek,
quick as lightning tongues of hummingbirds,
what's left when memory is all you are?

Bahia Hondo State Park

There's always someone last to jump.
It doesn't look so bad from down below,
from up above the rocks are hiding underneath the spray,
the cars are rushing on the bridge,
even though there's only thirty miles to go
before America comes dwindling to its end.
The water's flexing ligaments of dirty blue,
what a waste if now is when a tragedy ensues,
limp body carried in a dirty giant's hand.
But heads are bobbing, telling you to jump.
Everyone then gets into the car
and drives to where the sun is almost gone
and Mexico is squirting red into the sky.
Someone turns and points toward the east.
All of greasy Florida has flipped
and now there's only sliding into depths.
Night is black as oil and fills the throat.
How unexpected that it ends this way.

Carolyn Hembree

I am from New Orleans by way of Arizona, New York, South Carolina, Alabama, and Tennessee. "Wandering down the latitudes," as Dickinson describes in Poem 10, I finally put down roots in 2001. These twelve years in the Gulf Coast have rejigged my poetics so that my present work favors landscape over portrait, accretion over progression, and public as much as private address.

During the summer of 2005, I was writing a poem about the intersection of South Derbigny Street and Martin Luther King Boulevard for an anthology called Intersection (Press Street, 2006). Then, Katrina. When I returned to the city and "[O pony of South Derbigny o leaping yellow]" in October, I could not disentangle the many New Orleans—of my memory, my television screen, my present existence. So, I let all in.

While the Gulf Coast landscape has informed my subject matter, the religiosity of the Deep South has shaped my writing style. Throughout my childhood and adolescence in Tennessee and Alabama, I attended church weekly. Those prayers and litanies, apostate that I am, I can still recite. Of course, the old hymns, such as "Rock of Ages" and "I Love to Tell the Story," stir me, too. "Fox Ode" and "[O pony of South Derbigny o leaping yellow]" typify my brand of litany.

En route to my green bungalow, I can hear steamboats on the Mississippi, streetcars along Carrollton Avenue, the sirens, too. I pass the lurid hurricane shutters of my next-door neighbor. I smell the Confederate jasmine that I planted when pregnant with Mamie—heavy shrug of blossoms along my picket fence. I hope that these poems speak to and with this place and its denizens. For I feel that I have "to Eden wandered in—" Mine not a garden but a port city. Not so much *after* the fall. In the ecstatic and deadly *midst* of it.

[O pony of South Derbigny o leaping yellow]

O pony of South Derbigny o leaping yellow
on yellow pole carousel pony of South Derbigny
flooded pony o risen out of cobbled chimney of
shuttered mudhut of shutdown pawn shop
pony of South Derbigny   in attic windows
in amphibious tanks in Black Hawks in styrofoam
boats in whale-muraled vans in the alligator belly-
up on the highway pony of South Derbigny
pony of South Derbigny the airboat mother
her Gatorade her S earrings
her babying her baby   night-sky baby
blanket slipping off the slipping head
o yellow-crowned night-heron on the
upended light pole the golden
retriever in the black marsh the rotting
rottweiler on chain-
link pony of South Derbigny and stadium domes and sky-
lights of domes emptied of pony of South Derbigny emptied of
spotlights on boys mid-spree horsing and Boy Scout
knots across chests on gurneys   o gurneys of South Derbigny
slick jackets knotted at the waist
waist-deep in South Derbigny
chest-deep and dog-paddling
pony of South Derbigny past steeple bell speakers
past six headbanging hotel palms
pony of South Derbigny they crash
onto crashed Pontiacs
past umbrella oars past
hands waterlogged into papier mâché gloves raising the dead
reflected power line for reflected aluminum
              canoes to pass   past them all
pony of South Derbigny o pony of the mudhut floated into the street
       boy clothes still on the clothesline
pony of the thread count of those under sheets their feet jerking
       how can they still be jerking
pony of the body count   on baggage
carousels body on slate tiles in attics in lawn
chairs in short sleeves   the lawn chair in parking lots count on grass in sunflower
flip-flops in rubber banded cornmeal box shoes a girl I remember in shopping carts

wheelchair under a t-shirt veil count in off-the-shoulder hospital
gowns in uprooted black-rooted trees in prosthetic limbs   the limbs the souvenir boas
the dyed jet hair body in the long-pelted mink backless on chain-link in armoires
count in armories count in arms count
on buses on interstate ramps arms raised like a conductor against
the sky in cerulean housecoats with foam
white buttons I count exploding on South Derbigny
in one drenched sock hand-in-hand
body sighing on plywood in the air on knees Indian style on the airport floor
you pony of South Derbigny in an Indian beaded ghost
suit drying on the shredded screen door I remember
concentric rings in the flood water
cattle dog nosing   Black Hawk hovering
pony pony of South Derbigny you thing inside
the long yellow pelts of summer

New Orleans 2005

Fox Ode

So I'll leave this world

under a frost-tipped balding blue fox stole
under a *your-fiction-or-mine-big-boy* Mae West guardian angel

fox's guard for the wild foxy West, for the foxmade coast—
sunbathing foxes in French cut fox bikinis with silver tummy necklaces.

Just like us: one nicknamed Heaven, one with a metal detector
singing over the same de-stoned gumball ring. Just like us

foxes can flee their bodies a gazillion ways in the desert: foxholes,
fox hunts, fox mosh pits, fox tanning beds, foxes in bathtubs

with transistor radios, vampire foxes on breathing
machines to weird you out, but fox or no, can't we all plug into

one brand of breathing or other—mix flesh with a little voltage?
Science with fiction? With diction?

Some foxes fake their own deaths—a botched job—
one for a spread called *Dead Drunk Fox* (wink, wink):

motel pleather sofa bed, velvet superstar posters, Halloween
lipstick thumb-smeared to the chin. Other fox friends really are on ice:

a saggy-lidded Jean Harlow fox sidesaddle on a polar bear rug
its teeth showing, her chin cleft—*my sugar bowl sweetie*—

like Play-Doh that's been pinched.
Why do the best looking foxes always look a little like men? In midblow

Harlow fox's skirt makes an arctic circle.
An arctic circle around my margarita glass—

don't even bother salting that old wound, sweetie; suffering fox odes are deadly.
Try power ballads a cappella. Try air guitar. Lip synch on your barstool.

Who wouldn't dream of stealing limelight? Dream of springing forth like a birthday cake fox? Of outfoxing men with cheesecake? With fox trim?

I dream of hollow-boned flying like a spirit fox. Of saying to the pimp fox, Don't claw hammer my skull in two, not with all this confetti on my head.

Katherine Hoerth

This landscape is shaped by water, from raindrops that fall or don't, to the Rio Grande that slices through the earth, to the waves at the end where it all empties, sprawls, mixes, becomes one pool of salt and sand. On the South Texas coast, we live on the edges of worlds, but the gulf, the coast, reminds us that water isn't just a border where one ends, but a beginning, too, of something vast, beautiful, and maybe a little mysterious. I've spent many an afternoon contemplating this on the jettis of South Padre Island, just off the southern coast of Texas, staring across at al otro lado, the jagged rocks, no more jagged than the ones beneath my feet.

This contradiction, this thread of water, exists in language, too, and is reflected in the speech, the prose, and of course, the poetry of this region. There's a tension of water and land, of cultures, of language, of histories, of drought and flood. This spirit is what I hope my poems can encompass, can capture. Whether it's employing the flora of the region, the rocky textures of the language, the tensions between culturas, or a re-visioning of this landscape's folklore, the gulf, the end of land, the beginning of ocean, is very much alive in everything I write.

The Bull Rider

In Texas towns the tongues of men all taste
the same, like sour whiskey, dust between
the teeth. I think of this as neon lights
flicker above, my elbows on the bar.
A man sits down beside me, smells of sweat
and oil fields. He tucks his hands inside
his pockets, tells his story: he was once
a god on astroturf. I've heard it all
before, another song with steel guitar.
I lean in close and whisper in his ear:

I wanna ride a god right out this town.

He nods his head as though he understands.
I rise up from my stool and walk across
the boot scuffed floor, and mount the metal bull
that only drunken tourists ever try.
My fingers wrapped around the plastic horn,

I wave goodbye to his Aegean eyes,
the smell of smoke gives way to Padre breeze.
I kick my heels off, touch my naked toes
to froth. The metal bull between my legs
turns into flesh; the Coastal Bend recedes.

We ride all night to Crete, and I become
a woman even gods cannot resist.

"Adan y Eva" in the Rio Grande Garden of Eden

No matter the taste of the tongue – this story
doesn't change. The garden grew glorious

before the fall. Adan watches the pecan branches
reach up the tree's trunk from a crabgrass bed, aloe

awakened. He feels the wind curve the thick stems of Indian
blankets, and watches the pads of cow tongue cactus split

open at the bean pod flavor of mesquite. The faceless
Eva awaits, fading into the backdrop of paradise. She stoops

behind her Adan – his wild chest hair, his open
mouth grin, behind the swaying palm leaves,

shielding her eyes from his erect Adam's apple. It begs
Eva to cast away her veil of fronds, to show her face,

to take a bite. But until her bare toes mingle
among the blue sage brush – the crown-of-thorns

masking the pink spines of devil's head, she'll remain unnamed,
a hidden bloom in the prickly Rio Grande Garden of Eden.

Thomas Alan Holmes

It is difficult to express just what an impact the Gulf of Mexico had on me as a boy except to appreciate just how a limitless perspective of water and sky shaped my understanding of one's place in the world, not a sense of being small but a sense of wonder that there could be so much seemingly endless space. Today, as I work in southern Appalachia, I never see the horizon—every direction has a border of mountains and hills, trees and buildings. Here, we have to look up to see the sky. On the coast, one needs only look out. Even today, after the human-intensified suffering of Katrina and the calculated exploitation of the Deepwater Horizon catastrophe, I still see the Gulf as a challenge to be more than I am. As aware as I have grown of the need of stewardship of the region—it is much more delicate and responsive than its vastness suggests at first glance—I see it as an invitation to fulfill what potential I can imagine, knowing I will never fill that space between my place on the white sand and that blurred, indistinguishable far line between the sky and water.

Gulf Shores, 1968

At seven and nine, my brother and I
elbow prop, stomach down in the surf,
pink and brown from the sun, souvenir sailor caps
from the battleship moored in Mobile,

and our car is stuck. Dad digs in loose sand,
but the Pontiac's near bottomed out,
while our Mom keeps her vigil for riderless boards,
hint of undertow, and man-of-war.

Pascagoula

Pascagoula Easter Sunday
sunrise service, telling Mardi
Gras beads in my pocket, watching
sleepy, dressed-up children nestle
up against their parents, as my
small ones did, my bow-tied boys, my
ribboned girl, in patent leather
shoes with sleek, soft soles, I watch the
east for new horizon, any
hint of sun to pink the dogwood
petals. I can hear my voice in
song, "He lives! He lives!" remembered
words I cling to just outside this
prayerful circle, Easter Sunday,
Pascagoula, Mississippi.

Alice Johnson

I grew up below sea level. I could stand on the levee and watch the Mississippi coil brown and thick around New Orleans. My frame of reference changed the summer I stood on the sixty foot high white sand bluffs in Florida and looked down into the most beautiful ocean I'd ever seen: The Gulf of Mexico. The water blended from foam green, to dark blue and finally bled into a purple as it joined the greater ocean. Skidding down the sugary sand bluff towards the shore I heard a different sound under my feet almost like tennis shoes on a basketball court. The sand was so fine it felt sifted. Surf. I'd never seen that before either. Enticing white caps broke over distant sand bars and each piece of the bottom of the Gulf floor revealed new and more startling colors.

Unlike Lake Pontchartrain I could see creatures clearly, crabs burying themselves, needle fish darting through the tops of waves, off in the distance dolphin curled through the surf. It seemed I could wade out for a mile, the shallow depths lapping around my thighs as I grew accustomed to being one with the ocean.

As I stood waist high I remembered my first encounter with this piece of the sea as it carried its scent of sea oats and seaweed and with the bouquet came memories of tin buckets, small shovels and the distant sound of gulls swooping and diving. At first the birds frightened me with their shrill cries and then as I rocked into this new world I found the wind took away the strained pitch of their calls, softened them into a strand of notes, high and sweet, blowing out as far as I could see to the magical spot where water became sky.

Before Hurricanes Had Names

I am four. The world is criss-crossed
in tape and gnarled limbs, fallen and split
by a fierce, howling wind that sends
my daddy outside in his flapping purple bathrobe
as my mother cooks red beans, he slings his axe.
The kitchen is steamy, with shiny tall pots, hot with alarm,
and smells of dead ducks that lay defrosting on tile counter
tops their eyes are shiny as black patent leather like my shoes
in the closet where my grandmother is spared scary weather and stares
into rows of wool jackets and sweaters. She's peed in her chair
it dribbles in pools and I clean it up with bucket and water. Outside
is the sound of lines going POP,
boats clunking like bottles I've seen in the lake.

Gertrude our cook says this is the end. She's lighting candles
shouting prayers and amends
to her boyfriend the preacher outside on the stoop
scaling fish that stink just awful, need to be cooked.
My father unwraps vials of long needles
to shoot us with typhoid but my arm is too little so
I must bend over "the barrel" he says pull down my
pants and show him my butt. No water, no lights, rats run amok
on the wires, from Norwegian boats docked on the river
and still the rain falls in big sheets all silver.

The world has gone crazy is all I can figure.
Oaks bending and falling crashing right through the roof,
shingles sing by, whistle, like the birds gone missing,
I look out the window at branches nest-blown
and shredded and try to imagine just where they have hidden.
Down in the cellar the rats move right in and frighten us all
as they gnaw in our home. The radio stutters, clears its throat
and then dies and so does the world, the news from outside.
The mess, the mess, my mother is fretting while upstairs my grand-
mother
is lost in forgetting the clatter of garbage tops sailing and sailing.
Soon air becomes still, the sun pokes on down,
throw open the windows, fresh air returns,
but wires are still live, hot and unsafe, umbrella of sparks,
electrical snakes, but go to the closet, tell grandma it's safe,
it is now time to tear down the tape.

Gras Doux

Not the dictionary spelling, my
own choice to show the pedigree
of a New Orleans word meaning
grime, detritus, junk, extraneous
car crap, heaped clothing, fossilized
egg yolk on lapel, distilled bilge
water, congealed gravy, crawfish heads,
and other culinary Crescent City delights.

No question what it means
with the right inflection: "pick
up that gradoo." Or "don't leave
your gradoo all over the living room."
Words taste good in the Big Easy.
Take debris special, the gummiest

Beefy glutinous part of a po'boy sandwich.
Take the greeting where y'at? A state
of place and being. Banquette, to me a wet
sidewalk after a summer downpour;
an emerging moment of rain transforming
into mist. Make grocery conjures someone with a
meal in mind. The trinity: garlic, onions, bell peppers,
the marrow of Creole cooking
where cholesterol meets at the heart valves, clogging
like gutters in an August storm.

Whatcha know good? Says forget
any other gradoo. No time to
Fais do do, life's too rich for naps. The Parisiennes
have les rendezvous, cinq a sept,
but give me a calliope afternoon,
an Esplanade stoop, a long neck
Jax beer, a second line of waving
handkerchiefs and swinging backsides, umbrellas
twirling and the dead rising up to dance.

Julie Kane

Because I was born and raised in the Northeast and came to Louisiana only as a 24-year-old bride (having married a native), my poems display a "double consciousness" toward my adopted state and its Gulf Coast. The landscape will always be exotic and fascinating to me; I will never get used to seeing it, although I have lived here for more than half of my life. Reviewing my first book, *Body and Soul* (1987), Glenn Swetman wrote that "Kane, with her New England background, is able somehow to look at Louisiana in a way that picks out details a native might miss" (*Louisiana Literature*) and Norman German called me "Louisiana's petite de Tocqueville, for she surely allows us natives 'to see ourselves as others see us'" (*The Chiron Review*). You can see that they both picked up on that feature of my work.

Back then, not many poets native to this region were writing about it as a subject, but since Hurricane Katrina and the upsurge in awareness of our coastal erosion crisis, that situation has changed, because others have come to understand that the landscape is endangered, that it can be lost, that it is precious to them. In a sense, all of us Gulf Coast poets are "seeing double" now. It is no longer possible for any writer to take this place for granted.

At a very basic level, much of my work simply documents and celebrates the Louisiana landscape and its flora, fauna, and culture. At another level, though, my native Massachusetts and my adopted Louisiana take on polarities that are privately symbolic to me. Massachusetts is winter, snow and ice, rock and stone, the chilly Atlantic, hunger, emotional coldness, fate, judgmentalism. Louisiana is summer, tropical flowers and vegetation, ripeness, lushness, the Mississippi delta, wetlands, music, dancing, feasting, sensuality, love, forgiveness, grace, second chances.

Purple Martin Suite

> "I have had several opportunities, at the period of their arrival, of seeing prodigious flocks moving over [New Orleans] or its vicinity, at a considerable height . . . I walked under one of them with ease for upwards of two miles, at that rate on the 4th of February 1821, on the bank of the river below the city, constantly looking up at the birds, to the great astonishment of many passengers, who were bent on far different pursuits."
> —John James Audubon

1.
Any excuse, a holiday or death
will make them twirl umbrellas, shake their butts
to brass band music in the streets. I swear,
what won't these people make a party of?
So when my neighbor loaded beer on ice
and grabbed two folding chairs and said he meant
to go watch birds roost underneath a bridge,
it seemed no odder an excuse than Lent
to celebrate. We parked the pickup truck
by Entergy and slid down dirt banks under
girders where the Causeway Bridge meets land,
silenced by the rush-hour traffic's thunder
whizzing overhead. No sign, yet, of a bird:
I had to take my neighbor at his word.

2.
I had to take my neighbor at his word
that there would be a show, as birds arrived
in ones and twos and then in blue-black streams
to scribble meaninglessly on the sky,
thousands and thousands of them swarming; then,
as if an orchestra were tuning up,
the sun dipped under the horizon like
the fall of a baton, the "theater" hushed,
and suddenly the birds began to soar
in perfect loop-de-loops and barrel rolls,
whole squadrons of them flying synchronized
as vintage prop planes in an aircraft show,
till even those not mystically inclined
would swear they were connected mind to mind.

3.

As if they were connected mind to mind,
one group of them broke off and swooped en masse
below the Causeway, settling wing to wing
along steel girders; then a second pass,
a third, as any birds who hadn't found
a spot the last dive, flowed into the next,
the way a mother braids a daughter's hair
or villanelle picks up old lines of text.
When it was over it was way too dark
to tell their outlines from the sky or lake.
We stood and clapped as if we'd seen the Meters
reunited on a Jazz Fest stage,
joined beat to beat and holding in our breath
as night fell on that holiday from death.

Womanish Blues

Now a hurricane ain't no woman
and a steamboat ain't no bitch
Camille was no damn woman
and the Natchez ain't no bitch

Now America ain't no woman
but Louisiana is

She sure enough be womanish
Don't shove no map at me
You know the bitch be womanish
Don't shove no map at me

That river a slit, that delta
a woman's vee

Saturday girls on the porches
got them rollers in their hair
Saturday girls on the porches
all got rollers in their hair

Go for a drive and that pink
be everywhere

Shotgun house it suit me fine
Four rooms all in a line
Shotgun house it suit me fine
Wide as a bullet is wide

Shoot your ass dead on the porch
from back inside

Wind blow in from the bayou
comin' home like a guilty man
Funky wind from the bayou
comin' home like a guilty man

Don't let me smell that bayou
on your hand

Birch Thoughts in Louisiana

When I see birches bend to left and right,
shedding their bark in black and silver rings,
I think of martyrs being skinned alive.

Saint Bartholomew comes to mind,
holding, grim Santa, his sack of skin.
When I see birches bend to left and right,

someone in the family must have died
to get me on a plane up North again,
happy as a martyr skinned alive.

Here's the secret of a happy life:
Go where what's outside you fits what's in.
When I see birches bend to left and right,

silhouetted in December light,
bent over double, deathly thin,
I think of martyrs being skinned alive.

Winter, I think, is a long, dark night
of the soul, and snow is the wages of sin.
When I see birches bend to left and right,
I can't believe I made it out alive.

Greg Koehler

The sloughs and bayou, the mangroves obscuring the shore, the silty plains that spread out beneath the widening rivers. Palmetto, pine, live oak, cypress. The egrets and mockingbirds, the carolina wren in for a visit in the Spring. The rattlesnakes and water moccasins, the alligators basking on a blacktop road in the cold and dry season of winter. Oil rigs and refineries glowing by the freeway like a city of glittering spirits. Lumps of beach tar stuck to the bottom of my calloused feet. The Seminole, the Calusa, the Karankawa, the Comanche, the Chitimacha, the Creek. The Cajuns, the Creole, the Crackers, Austin's Old Anglo Three Hundred. The stern Spanish Jesuits in their missions, curious Mexicans wandering back up into places that feel old and new, familiar and foreign.

These are the stories, the people, the trees, and waters I have grown up with, their sights and the rich and varied tongues that speak about and through them. They have stained and polished my imagination and my language for the bulk of my life. From my roots and chosen home of Texas to my high school years in gulf-coastal South Florida, with various stints in South Louisiana, I have spent my life in the south, along the Gulf Coast, listening to these voices.

Alabama River Dirge

If it's not too much to ask, may a black
man sit on the porch ignoring the sweat
collecting in and on his shirt and brow.

Our casual piety demands, at the very
least, a bow, an arrow, and a remember:
there is bread before the toast, wheat

before the bread, sun and soil and water
and farmer before the wheat, woman
toasting bread before the farmer rises.

When we line our eyes with red war paint,
I think I hear a drum beat, but you say it
is an air conditioner. Is a rapid construct,

a rural studio. Square and rectangle, you
violence you lust you stop dead in your
tracks, sun in the drops of sweat on their

backs. Barn swallows, Rita Marley, Haile
Selassie and Cynthia Wesley. Electrical
storm, summer jubilee Mobile Bay, you

disregard.

Atchafalaya River Dirge

You eighty-six cicadas, I can't stand
it anymore. I can't pole my old pirogue
through the darker bayous with your
endless butt-shake rattle-rattle. God-

damnit Eighty-Sixers, I can't take hat
in hand without the rattle.
                             I name you,
all eighty-six of you, for it is only right
to call out and name the blasted sect
before dealing in just condemnation.

Shit. Can't lace up my shoes, Pilgrim
can't get any goddamn rest. You're like
bricklayers climbing the celibacy tree, like
Jesuits on the bullhorn at the racetrack.

Like pigs in the thistle, like the preacher's
sweethearts. Like March mockingbird
chick chirps an hour before dawn.

Now Pilgrim's dead above ground, lifted
by and wrapped in cypress knees. Your
song is still the rattle of my failing mettle,
still my pirogue sunk in the black bayou.

Mississippi River Dirge

Cantilevered over turbid waters
on the Gramercy Bridge, I lean
out over the railing and breathe
this ancient invocation:
You are like the Mississippi.

With and between the banks,
bear-shaped burial mounds
marching, your brackish waters
carry salt and tangles of brush.
Wild-eyed Indi'ns and common

loons paddle. Coal slurry.
Cow shit. Rusted barges commit
shiny slicks of gasoline to your
buzzing surface. Violet light
sunburns suspension bridge

and beaver skeletons. They rust
and rot like beard trimmings
in the drain catch. Giant gar feed
on carrion. Nutria dig, compromise
the levees. Murmur and smirk.

Abandoned vessels float and
sink, bilge and mildew. Among
them yours, and soon mine.

John Lambremont, Sr.

Even a cursory look at my poems will reveal my Gulf South roots immediately. Many of them are about my native south Louisiana, the Southern jewel that is New Orleans, the excesses of Texas, the Gold Coasts of Alabama and Florida where we vacation, and the geography, customs, and traditions of the region.

The region provides a rich cornucopia of ideas for poems about local and indigenous people, music, food, festivities, environs, institutions, and culture. We have endured much here, including natural disasters and man-made fiascoes, the ravages of Reconstruction and the struggles of desegregation, and corrupt local governments and uncaring administrations; yet, we abide and take solace in a still-wonderful way of life that allows us to work hard and prosper and live large and relax resplendently.

It doesn't matter whether one is the descendant of a former slave, a Baton Rouge blue blood, a Livingston Parish redneck hippie with a mullet, or a "Yat" from New Orleans' Ninth Ward, almost all here share in the pursuit of the good life available, whether it be in hunting or fishing, drinking wine and fine dining, or our near-insane fervor for barbecue and football.

The Gulf Coast flavors its residents as surely as Zatarain's crab boil flavors boiled seafood and fixings, and poems from writers of the region, even those in the finest institutions of higher learning, share a unique and distinct aroma and flavor that are encapsulated into the work like a Cajun spice injection into a fried turkey, permeating throughout and unmistakable in origin.

The Wood Grows Silent

I had stood alone for so long,
watching my deciduous forest grow,
that the first filing seemed a relief,
as children are more lively
than are rabbits and moles.

Homes too hot to stay in,
yards too hot to play in,
kids took refuge in the parasol
of my broad-leafs' shadows,
an ancient noble live oak
the center of the compass
of my known world.

Its vine became a swing
across a ravine and back,
its wide roots platforms
for making the leap.
Boards nailed into its huge girth
made rungs to climb up
to broad branch benches.
The boys made bike paths
in and around the valley,
and a campsite developed
at the height of the upper loop.

My lagoon taught the children
about water striders and dragonflies,
terrapins and moccasins,
and my meadow was full of dandelions
and dewberries ripe for picking.
The boys chopped and stripped thistle
for the crunchy inner ring,
and the girls gathered acorns for
biscuits and sought chanterelles
under the shaded ivy of slopes.
But, as the great poet once said,
"Nothing gold can stay,"
and slowly things changed.

Boys were smoking grapevines,
then stolen cigarettes, a careless match
burning up half my meadow
one hot and dry August day.

Stick guns became air rifles,
and play forts became shanties built
from stolen construction materials.
Bad boys took foolish girls
under the boughs, out of sight,
for mawkish attempts at intercourse,
and later, three deranged brothers
took the autistic boy up the old oak
and used his arms for an ashtray
and his head for a urinal.

By then, the houses had window units,
and the kids were forbidden to enter me,
and stayed away. Once again I stood alone,
until the second filing came.

My meadow, ravine, and lagoon
were all bulldozed and leveled,
and the sacred oak of centuries
was toppled and set ablaze.
But a part of me remained,
a secret to a lucky few,
beyond a hedge of cane-brake,
a large cypress swamp-lake
of more than forty acres,
a place of egrets and alligators
and quiet.

That part of me is preserved
as a city-owned wildlife center,
with overlooks and walkways,
and a hall with bright-lit exhibits;
my park bears the bluebonnets' name.

Chip Livingston

I was raised in northwest Florida and grew up on the beaches and rivers of coastal Alabama and Florida, which have influenced everything about myself, from my identity as a Poarch Creek Indian to the rhythms and content of my verse.

Burn

That owl was an omen
Driving home from the airport
Not once but twice
It rose in my headlights
From rain black asphalt
Great white wings nearly touching
Windshield wipers   that low flying escort
Stretching sixty miles toward Alabama
The owl was always right
Something died and something else
Was just about to
I checked my daughter's red-eye slumber
In the rearview mirror
No need to worry her with divination
An hour drive delayed by rain
And now this trepidation on the slick black road
Certain as miscarried fortune
Her coming home to Mama in an autumn storm
And no such thing as California
Just a red clay creekbed down the road
From the house I birthed her in
Filling up to bathe away a sorrow
Blinking lights behind us
Before I hear the sirens
Firetruck passes on the narrow bridge
Then Crabtree Church in flames beyond the graveyard
My daughter wakes and guesses lightning
But I never heard the thunder crack
And only saw the lightning white of dreaded wings
I pull in   step out open an umbrella
Stand with the firemen   watch the frame fall down
The Marshall asks if we saw anything
Like kids driving away in a four-wheeler
They found tracks in the mud
Whiskey and beer bottles   a gas can
Burn! All those years of homecoming
Annual dinners on the grounds
Hymns around a weather-warped piano
Burn! My granddad's Indian education

Walls that heard a thousand lessons
A thousand prayers in high soprano
Burn! Fifty paper funeral parlor fans
Cokesbury hymnals and sixteen pews
Reduced to flakey carbon tamped with rain
The death of wood and glass
And half a baby's ashes in my daughter's pocketbook
All the little names we'll never sing
I aim to find that messenger again and scare him off
Litter the road with his insolent feathers

Defuniak Springs

Ready with the minute hand,
walking the shore of isn't asked,
among cypress mud, little knees shrugging
their watch, the crappie bedded
in pebbled water, us mumbled
by their congregation, by
what swayed forth, assumptions
mussing the whispered shoulder,
the fist-sized thought, head testing
the crisis reached – we stumbled
into symptoms, shadows
turning water into turning water,
the stumpknockers' spasms liquid
against root, against autumn,
and just before we turned into roads,
your eyes were wide as a cottonmouth's strike
feeling the quake of a step,
and nature completed the truth of the matter,
stomached a subject unalterable:
We were four-footed, with appropriate clouds,
and how much like gravestones
were your slate buttons.

Cleopatra Mathis

Even in north Louisiana, I felt I lived in a land of water—hiding the land or hiding just beneath the land—ever present, insidious. You had to watch where you stepped. Swamp and bayou: the first downright tricky with its quicksands and rot, teeming with creatures, and the other more orderly. Even the name "bayou" implied the grace of color, the distinct water marked by cypress trunks, water plants, mosses. The place I liked for its names, for the fishing, and in open areas, the swimming. I was a child who longed for the ocean I'd seen in pictures: clearly defined water rushing up against land, a pristine border of white sand, then withdrawing. It was pure emptiness, pure noise, fixed by the timing of tides. The sound I lived with was a blur of buzz, squeak, rattle, chirp, a gentle cacophony rising and falling. The birdsong, too many kinds to distinguish between them, never stopped in any season, background to every hour. I woke to utter dark and still they twittered on, companion to my sleep. And the deluge of rain, sideways sheets of it, the roads washed out. The dull color of the air, heavy with water. Spring through summer, straight down the state, parish by parish, the rivers overflowed, the jagged, submerging Gulf threatening to take it all.

This was long ago in a rural place where now there is a super highway just yards from our old front door. D'Arbonne Swamp, the thirty or so miles of it, is the new north side of town with its good neighborhoods and schools, and beyond that, D'Arbonne State Park, everything lethal and teeming and true to itself drained away, dug out, sanitized: a civilization of azaleas, an insistent cultivation. Once, I waded and dodged and feared my step, but in the end found wild persimmons, a gold tree whining with a thicket of wasps. As they gorged, they let me through; I had my share.

The Faithful

In the hierarchy of things to-see, the larger
stones come last, then the moss or lichen-covered
near water, and the routine
glide of minor birds in the path of vision.
Because the eye's accuracy is approximate,
squirrels weigh less than rabbits. And because we like
what disappears, deer count most, though foxes
bring a certain gift if accidentally
glimpsed at sunrise in an open field.
Deer on the road at night mean to tell you
something's lost: my embryonic first child
did not survive the omen of a five-point buck
crossing the midnight road before us. And though I slept,
head in my husband's lap the rest of the way home,
we would be split forever by our ways
of seeing that grief.

What I grew up seeing as a wall of green
is really a thousand species of the rare
and seldom seen. The average swamp
is a death of stumps and snakes
the eye teases from the submerged
vegetation, hardly knowing what's imagined
from what the brown water covers. So I look now
past the lie of broken cypresses,
the scum and sludge of those static limbs,
to swamp fishing with my silent mother,
night crawlers and the bag of macaroni at her feet.
I know she counted lucky our winters rich with fish
hovering in the water's buggy heat
and the accident of common need
that brought us to the birds.
Hunched over in the prow, brooding into dawn,
I saw them without attention: one generic white
as they gathered, an occasional red
detail on the crest of a neck.
What came exact were the bottom eaters,
cat and bream, trashfish
whose bloody gills and writhing I still see
plain as day in the bottom of the boat.

She could wait for hours,
devoted to the hidden: a glimpse
of the nested blue-veined
eggs among the stink of the water hyacinths
catching at our boat, those fake orchids
buoyed up like bladders on their leaf stalks.

Now rounding a bend near an opening in the pines
where a mass of tiny buttercups
dot the weeds, I barely catch sight of
a dozen or so goldfinches darting up,
themselves like flowers someone has thrown.
That kind of seeing is enough
to keep me for a week. With other birds
even the names determine sight:
bittern and cormorant for their shyness
or the ghostly rattle of a kingfisher
making a certain claim on us in exchange
for visibility. I've tripped on the running path,
thinking folded leaves were wings,
and even what I don't witness can stop me cold:
evidence of a jay, jab by jab,
tearing to pieces a rose finch still in the nest.
But we disregard the penalty for seeing,
just as we think we see in birds
our own possibilities for grace;
our only touch is with tongue and teeth
in the syllables of their lovely names.
And because each one of us has flown in dreams
we dreamed perhaps just once, those wings for us
precede words, precede the logic
of how things rise. Some pinion
connects who we are with whatever pulls us
to walk into the evening's wetland grasses
in an air made of sounds we listen for,
a hearing that reveals what rises hoping
for the scarlet ibis and the blackcrowned,
that catalog of all the herons,
the grace of seeing that will save us.

On a Shared Birthday: J. C. L. 1953-1979

Now with another year I save
his battered case with the driller's glove
and spearmint gum, salt worn, stiff the
modern sailor's two week stint
in the pull for oil out in the Gulf.
Roughnecker's gig of bad food, bad sleep,
the six hour drive down Louisiana's spine,
rain all the way to the measured
whistle of daywork, nightwork,
work and wake at 3 a.m. And I see again
what I never saw: my brother timing the seconds against
losing his hand as he centers the steel
under the hammer's flying weight
that jams the rod into the ocean floor ...

I pull myself up,
back to dawn and the single bird note, sustained
stop and start like worry.
Face into sheet, I nag
red-winged blackbird, more naming
to sidestep panic, as if that whistle
could make sense of a life that's missing.
What's this birthday now
but the baggage of injury and pardon two
landscapes and one bird
crossing them night after night.
Where, where, where, it sings,
is your brother now? In this dream
no death, no murderer's
hand on my brother's throat. No body
dumped in the convenient swamp, the convenient rain
that goes on washing away.
The litany of what we'll never know
comes to nothing but the haunting in one bird's song.

Out of the chirp and chatter,
the hundreds I can or can't name, it's unrecognizable
in the manual I took from his things lost
in the lovely words like pinion,

the heart of a wing, diagrams
of red and white flight muscles, the mechanical
swoop of landings. How else, he said,
to while away the time
in a bunk at the boat's bottom, too nervous to sleep
the eight hours off. Now this bird
hovers over my sleep and when I run
it travels. A bad morning means I resist
its cipher, half song in half light,
and the road drags at my feet.
I run to hear nothing but the pulses beat,
to coax some flutter of my own.
Still inside sleep the call
is maddening, always over there.
I stumble into the field where those three notes
elude and carry, where the mower has gone.
The grass lies down like water
in a picture, caught this way and that.
In its wake the simple carnage of a mouse,
back neatly sliced, then three eggs, scattered.
It begins to rain. I go on finding these bodies.

Salt Water Ducks

The tide ignores its limits, all last night
climbing over the railing, battering the door.
White spume flew its ghost against the glass.
The bay's in its third day of outrage,
but the ducks have to eat. The white-winged scoter
keeps me at the window, three sleek ones.
I count the in and out of their pristine heads—
bodies down for improbable minutes
before coming back up, black and white
against the white-capped black water shoving
against the row of stone pilings that mark the tide's high rise.
By 8 a.m. I've seen enough
as the rocks submerge and the overwrought current,
something like a boxer pounding and pounding,
slams the ducks diving there—I've seen enough

to know what I'll find tomorrow on the wasted beach:
a washed-up duck, still intact,
limp sack beneath the flawless design
of its feathers, nothing odd except the crumpled pose.
Audubon propped them up on wires, a scaffold of bird—
no other way to capture life than to show it dead.
Brutality not part of art's equation, we like to think.
Meanwhile, the birds are all instinct
in the moment. This life in a wild wind
is only the din they live in. I doubt they even hear it.

Karla Linn Merrifield

Over the past twenty years, I have been creating a body of poems rooted in place. To write these poems, I first experience specific habitats (e.g., the Everglades, Badlands, Okefenokee Swamp, Utah Canyonlands, Antarctica), observing them with a naturalist's as well as a poet's eye and sensibility. I inhabit the place, it inhabits me, and then I translate my findings into poems.

In the process I make new discoveries about the nature of nature – and man's role in it, both historically and in the present day – ones that are sometimes told from the point of view of another species or natural entity (e.g., a dolphin, a torreya tree, a stone, a river, a dewdrop). In addition, since the first Earth Day in 1970, when as a senior in high school I represented my school at the New York State Legislature's celebration of the day, I have been a student of Rachel Carson; her *Silent Spring* thoroughly influenced my life as poet and citizen of the Earth. I've been a committed environmentalist and a poet with an environmental trajectory ever since.

Perhaps the greatest evidence for that is *The Dire Elegies: 59 Poets on Endangered Species of North America,* an anthology I edited (with my husband) for FootHills Publishing in 2006. And now, as a Gulf Coast resident of several years (North Fort Myers, Florida), my poems have more often focused on the fragile Gulf Coast, most often taking a pro-environmental stance and seeking to inspire readers to live a more ecologically engaged life as stewards of the Gulf Coast. The poems, several of which have been published in Alabama's *Steel Toe Review* (search archives online) also embody my belief that poetry furthers the sacred and that there is nothing more sacred than preserving the Coast, the planet.

1564: The Virgin One

If an Everglades goddess reigns,
she is a Calusa spirit,
a woman of oyster mounds—
the pearl who never saw
the glinting Spanish
hack a kingdom out of bones.

And she is the limestone full moon,
clasped by slash pines;
she is the purple gallinule,
a rainbow of gems in the marsh.
She is the prairie's opalescent periphyton,
mother of all.

She is the gold river of grass;
she is the silver, liquid light.

The ABCs of Everglades Hurricanes

The alphabet of natural disaster begins again
each June: A as in Andrew.

Since the '50s, we name all hurricanes
that rage across this liquid land
that is southern Florida.
We remember the most destructive hurricanes,
hurricanes for the history books,
hurricanes for the records of man.

We recall that Isbell rearranged
the Ten Thousand Islands
on her whirlwind trip in 1964.
Inez, '66, the crazy one, zigzagged
her path of slaughter through the Keys
and then ensued Alma, Gladys, Abby.
The '60s rocked on and along came Donna:
Goodbye mangroves, goodbye white herons.

Down at Flamingo, it was only a matter of time,
thirty-some years of calm, before another murderous blow.
What Donna didn't finish
in the black forest of the coast in '68,
Wilma did in 2005.
In her deadly wake of storm surge and salt intrusion,
the Eco-Pond is going, going, almost gone.
The lodge: blown out, washed out,
doorless, windowless concrete hulk.
The maniac had done her ghost-town work.

We recite a litany of ravishment
from Madeira Bay, to Cape Sable, up to Chokoloskee,
where Lostman's River keeps getting lost.
We track, we monitor, we enter data.
We author articles and books.
We issue treatises and master plans.
We write poems.
And we wonder why hurricanes are getting worse.
Will a year come when we run through our ABCs
and call the last and worst one Zora?

Learning the Tide Tables of Grief

Where the Southern Everglades meets the sea,
tide is the medium; all our comings
and goings out into the Gulf, downstream
to estuaries, into bays, wherever the eye goes,
we are ruled by the spring and neap, by moon phases.
And it is low water now, friend, low water
in this tropical place and in your heart.

A few days from now, a few weeks—soon—
your father will die and you will be orphan child.
But you will be wise enough
to listen with me to the waves lapping
at countless roots, then letting go,
retreating, but returning and returning.
You will hear it said by the tides:
Life goes on after death.

As in Paradise, distances are immeasurable in
the Southern Everglades.
This place deals in earthly eternities;
the dead lie in the open.
This is vulture country, but living goes on
in the tropical land of your heart.

Because it is low water now, friend, low-water's
slack tide of exposed oyster beds and sand banks,
the channel is treacherous.
Wait with me; be still.
Time will come—soon—for tears.
Time will come—soon—to take up
the current and follow its flow.

for Katie McDonald

Benjamin Morris

As a native of Hattiesburg, Mississippi, I spent my childhood on the gulf coast—in Gulfport and Biloxi, in New Orleans, with family in Pensacola, and most often, fishing and boating with my father in the Pascagoula river town of Vancleave, Mississippi. After years overseas in graduate school (during which I studied the impacts of Hurricane Katrina on the culture of New Orleans and the Gulf South), I returned home to live and write here full-time. My work most frequently centers on place, and the uniqueness of place—one collection in progress focuses on an endangered hardwood forest in Louisiana, begun while in residence at A Studio in the Woods, and another is a book which envoices the state highways of Mississippi, starting along the coast and working north. I'm still on the coast, living in New Orleans and working in Mississippi as a member of the state Artist Roster, writing and teaching, and working on a new history of my hometown, Hattiesburg.

Highway 49 (to Gulfport)

They say that lightning forked her years ago
but I wouldn't know. I'm not that old.
Despite the fact that I run straight to coasts
of sand and oil and wrack and that I could
not have been built soon enough, she outpaced
me by years. Decades, if that's what you want
to call them. It wasn't exactly a race
that we ran together but she won it
anyway, standing tall, then twice tall,
once the blast cracked her in half—and then
she cast her net of shade on all
of us, even the bushhog that they sent
to eat her roots alive, to widen me—
where now she sounds, a tuning fork, inside me.

~~D~~ay 26 *(to Wiggins)*

~~I~~ ~~am~~ is longer than your eyes can see.
Its edge extends past the road on which
you drive, deep into the spine of history
where men grew famous, fat and rich
for how many acres they could fell in a day.
I was born of the need to bring the pines
westward, to clear a cleaner way
through this ancient thicket for the lines
of trucks and railcars that would follow.
They cut me first, and now I cut them back:
leaving pyramids of timber logs stacked
like matchsticks, hundreds of feet and taller.
Hewn, hauled, corded, piled and sold:
the elders of this forest, untold centuries old.

Brent Newsom

I lived the first eighteen years of my life--born and raised, as the saying goes—in the small town of DeRidder, Louisiana, seat of Beauregard Parish and, at one time in my youth, proud home of the first Walmart Supercenter in the state. When new acquaintances find this out, they often note with surprise that I have no trace of a "Louisiana accent." Whether the accent they mean is Cajun or Creole or redneck or what I never know. I assure them a Southern drawl does slip out occasionally, when I'm around extended family. This dialectal code-switching is a way of adapting to my environment, I suppose, one that happens more or less unconsciously and, I believe, serves as an apt metaphor for my relationship to my home state: I love it and "speak its language," but except for occasional visits, I've left it behind.

Nevertheless, the place and its people exerted a profound influence on me. In my youth I experienced this influence as unconsciously as I later experienced my changes in elocution. But just as a fish knows when it is no longer in the water, absence from a place has a way of bringing its uniqueness to light. I really became aware of the distinctive characteristics of my hometown and state, deeply impressed on me though they were, only after living in other places. In response, I created the fictional town of Smyrna, an amalgam of Louisiana towns and cities where I have lived or otherwise enjoyed and endured formative experiences. Then, in poetic mini-narratives, I peopled the town with individuals like Esther Green and Floyd Fontenot, people whose lives are tinged with the economic, religious, political, racial, and even moral tensions that, in my new awareness, seemed simultaneously particular to Louisiana and universal. Writing these poems felt like a compulsion—or perhaps a duty—as well as an opportunity to once again speak the local language.

Smyrna

By a strip of highway spilled beside a swamp
that exhales sphinx moths and hums mosquito hymns:
their kids sack out on sofas while the men
make sweatless love to tired wives, then go
perspire in oil-smeared, orange hard hats
on caffeinated graveyard shifts. Days off,
they jaw across their truck beds lined with cans
in the gravel lot outside the donut shop.
Come winter, dawn and dusk, they tramp the bogs
with shotguns, taking life as it comes to them.
Pass through and you'll be met with friendly waves
and icy stares. At the edge of town, by the caution light,
a metal sign, green, lettered in white:
WELCOME — riddled with steel shot.

Esther Dreams of Floyd for the Third Straight Night

So many reasons this is wrong—
he's much too young for me,
I'm six short months a widow…
But he comes to me again,
this time in a lowland forest
where wildflowers open to drink
the dew, scents of cypress and pine
rise, and gray limbs sift the lazy sunlight
playing across my paisley bed.
On a stump: a stoneware carafe,
a green bar of Lava,
Granny's ceramic basin
—bone-dry on the dresser for decades,
it held Bill's wallet and smokes.
Overhead, wind rustles Spanish moss
like the hair of some woodland fairy.

I take Floyd by the bicep,
lead him to the stump.
I pick up the carafe and pour
until the basin is full, take the soap
and wash away the engine grease
from Floyd's thick, heavy hands,
which then leave their wet prints
on my hip and back. I slip
each blue button of his shirt
through its hole, a row of keys
unlocking a door to the secret
garden in a book I once read
to my girls. His kisses
taste of pecan pie
as we fumble toward the bed.
He likes the softness of my body.
Our clothes have disappeared,
I'm locked in the curves of his arms
when I hear the crunch of leaves underfoot
and I push Floyd away, fold into myself
like a morning glory at midnight.
I'm curled tight beneath the sheet,

in tears, when at the foot of the bed,
there's Bill, a Winston slung between his lips,
the fishing line strung from his cane pole
vanishing into Granny's basin
as if it held an entire lake. The cane tip
bobbles and dips, and Bill pulls out a fish,
a good-sized bluegill. Carefully,
he wraps his hand around the fish's fins,
then pulls from its stuttering mouth
a silver coin. He drops the fish into the carafe,
then flips the coin with his thumb,
snatches it out of the air, grins,
and says, Go on, Queenie, it's all right by me.

That's when I wake, alone and small
in our queen-sized bed. I pull
to my face the faded bedspread, inhale
the odor — barely there — of cigarettes.

Deborah Paredez

For so many of us who grew up as working class Tejanos, the Gulf was so near and so far. The place to try your luck on the gambling boats or to escape from it on the pounded shore. The place where the view of the refineries—lit up and emptied of promises like Oz—was clearer than the view of the coastline. The place that held us at once in its thrall and in its undertow, that held contradictions, that taught us to live them. Today, it's the place where the Selena memorial stands, sea-worn and laden with our offerings, our regrets and longings. The place of pilgrimage and the place to leave behind. The way the poem is both the landmark I seek and the street sign receding in the distance as I write my way home.

The Gulf, 1987

The day upturned, flooded with sunlight, not
a single cloud. I squint into the glare,
cautious even then of bright emptiness.
We sit under shade, Tía Lucia
showing me how white folks dine, *the high life*.
I am about to try my first oyster,
Tía spending her winnings from the slots
on a whole dozen, the glistening valves
wet and private as a cheek's other side,
broken open before us. *Don't be shy.*
Take it in all at once. Flesh and sea grit,
sweet meat and brine, a taste I must acquire.
In every split shell, the coast's silhouette:
bodies floating in what was once their home.

Elegy for Donald Clark, Assistant Driller Newellton, Louisiana, 2010

More in the ground than in school around here.
He worked a decade on the rig, always
seemed to be leaving even when he was
home, walking hours in the pecan groves,
crushed catkins ochreing the ground beneath
him. The gym not been this full since before
the mill shut down and all the white folks left.
Undertow of Interstate Sixty-five,
the ones left rising for another hymn.
To the east of town is an oxbow lake
named for St. Joseph, patron of workers.
Years since the lake took shape — wide meander
of the Mississipp — sealing itself
from its source, no longer serving the sea.

us Christi

Paycheck cashed and four-thirty Friday
bus to Corpus Christi's beckoning tides —

tied scarf keeping our bouffant's lift
on the boardwalk stroll   swooping

gulls and their squawks
buckets of shrimp bought right

off the boat, boiled 'til those pink
skins slip off easy as a loose girl's

stockings on Saturday night — what salvation
was   a weekend with sand

dollars the size of the Eucharist
filling our pockets.

Alison Pelegrin

In my life there is no escaping the Gulf of Mexico, not that I would want to. I grew up in New Orleans, which means that there is a healthy fear inside of me of hurricanes and what they might do to the Mississippi River. It always seemed to me that the levees kept the water back by holding it over our heads.

In my family, many of the men worked offshore on oil rigs or fished for a living. On weekends, when they were on shore, we'd drive the coast to Biloxi to sightsee, eat fried seafood, or visit the Oceanarium. We vacationed then, and still do, in Pensacola, Florida. Each of these places has been inexplicably altered by hurricanes and oil spills.

I mourn the coast—permanently altered, but also recovering—like I mourn the family members who first brushed its sand from my toes.

Pantoum of the Endless Hurricane Debris

I drive the Gulf Coast to get away,
but this Mississippi debris seems familiar.
What's left is front steps leading nowhere,
the watermark, oak trees trimmed with car parts.

This Mississippi debris seems familiar.
Plywood everywhere. I need some time off
from watermarks and oak trees trimmed with car parts.
Debris shingles my memory lane.

Plywood everywhere. I need time off.
There's a yellowed snapshot of me here.
Debris shingles my memory lane,
no landmarks left. Where am I again?

There's a snapshot of me here, or close to here,
with a sea lion planting kisses on my cheek.
No landmarks left. Where am I again?
What happened to the Oceanarium?

Once, a sea lion kissed me on the cheek.
Dolphins rode out the storm in swimming pools.
What happened to the Oceanarium?
The storm surge clawed it out to sea?

Dolphins rode out the storm in swimming pools.
The gift shop, where dad bought me a jewelry box,
the storm surge clawed it out to sea.
On Sundays we used to picnic here.

Dad bought me a cedar jewelry box.
The air smells sweetly of hurricane debris.
On Sundays we used to picnic here,
landscape of front steps leading nowhere.

Hurricane Party

No way in hell the sky would do me wrong.
Even with the weatherman keening
in his yellow slicker, it just doesn't sink in.

Plywood, shrimp boots, sandbags, and booze.
Stuck in line at the hardware store,
pancakes for dinner after schools close early.
Before landfall, before the water comes
and anyone gets hurt,

        it's always fun—
chanting the alphabet of past hurricanes
that never harmed besides a muck mosaic
in the streets,

        the waterline's footprint
a jagged hem of leaves on the lawn.

Taping the windows, packing
for a midnight exodus, our map
the lava flow of headlights. In the car—
pillows, a coffee can for pee,
and *Michael, row the boat ashore.*

The aggravation makes the worst you've heard
seem not so bad, not even boating
from rooftop to rooftop after Betsy,

or cousin Chancy in the crook of a tree
delivered by a voice speaking out of the light:
Over here—*dis child, he cold.*

Is it chance, or is God listening when I beg
to be passed over, for someone to take my place
ripping up carpets and breathing the stench
of minnows shriveled on concrete?

Cameron Parish, Yucatan Peninsula,
the whole of Florida, Dominican Republic—
apologies for the times my blessings

have arrived at your expense—
 a feast of outage-thawed seafood,
the easy work of peeling tape
from crossed-off windows,

each pane scraped clean
a day the calendar is giving back.

Ode to the Pelican

Brown or white, you are the goofiest of birds.
Bird of crash dives and the infinite wattle,
creature most likely to be caricatured

in blown glass, to be carved and clown-painted
in Oaxaca. Albatross of the Gulf, usherer in
of fishing boats, even the psalmist took note:

I am like a pelican of the wilderness. Oh, my soul,
if I could shape shift, it would be you, pelican,
and I'd yawp from your roomiest of throats.

Pelican, Pelegrin: on lazy tongues our names alike.
Wing man of my father as he marathoned across
Lake Pontchartrain with blood in his shoes.

Portrayed prolifically in water colors, but rarely
the topic of a tribal tattoo. Selfless Pelican,
in stained glass second only to the dove,

feeding your trinity of flightless young with shreds
of flesh and sips of your own blood. On the state flag
they've sanitized your cannibal love, Louisiana bird.

What can we do for you, pelican? Oil spoiled,
washing up on toxic beaches. Marbled eggs
unforming while pious, blackened pelicans sit.

I have been faithless, pelican. All my life I thought
you were falling—reckless, sprawled like Icarus—
until you surfaced with a fish. Blue-gloved hands

hold you kindly in a tub, flush saline in your eyes,
give your feathers a toothbrush scrub. You fight
by giving up, unwilling or unable to be saved by us.

Bin Ramke

Although I was born on the Texas side of the Sabine River I spent much of my youth in or near Abbeville—more specifically, along the Vermillion Bayou, watching crew boats from the oil rigs travel too fast, their wake washing away the edges of my grandfather's farm, my father's birthplace. The longer I live in Colorado, my current geographical location, the more I need to understand the solubility of boundaries. Even my mother's Cajun speech was a challenge, a refusal to reside in English or French, but always in both, each dissolving, solving for some variable. Poetry inhabits the uncontrollable liminal, and by inhabiting declares a certain love—for instance, it is through making poems I came to understand how the etymology of cloud and clod are the same – the phase changes between solid and gaseous states are a kind of intercourse that living on the Gulf coast allowed me to witness daily. Most often I did not see the water, nor the land: I saw the clouds strictly aligned, a horizon, a lineation.

Resonance

> In 1938 John Cage composed a piece for the U.C.L.A. swimming team's annual water-ballet. Because vibrations through air are impeded by water, Cage experimented with gongs, lowered into the water, which could be heard by the swimmers.

> *Analysis of Newton's Method to Compute Travelling Waves in Discrete Media*, H.J. Hupkes and Verduyn Lunel: "We present a variant of Newton's method for computing traveling wave solutions to scalar bistable lattice differential equations. We prove that the method converges to a solution…"

To hear voices means to hear not-voices.
The perturbed human hears clear instruction
so follows it — what could be simpler.

Beneath the fluid medium the men and boys
buoyant and benign obey signals serving
the master, dancers doing what dancers do

among school children, dreaming of bodies
in a fit of rage or grief. Imagine a leaf floating
in the pool, the boys below listening

to gongs, the vibrant water washing tears
away the bloom of bodies swaying to music
as to the glance of light pooling below.

The floor of the swimming pool glittery
with sun and sound, unsound devices
divide each dancer from his dance.

Devices divide, and long afterward
little humans live their lingering lives —
it is called *decay,* a straying of attention.
Nuns and mothers listen to light.

Among the Functions of Flowers

Here we would live, and near the woods
to wander after dinner. A family full
glittered in moonlight

sultry. I was one among them
and while it never happened it mattered,
"matter" as verb, a making of material

things, the lumbering into furniture and futures.
We walked on land we called
ours, and the time it took to cross it

was a lie, lovely sylvan. Tree, oak,
live (adjectival pronunciation)
there was once a place and time

in the mind of a child verdant
the child made the greenness of the time
a function of mind in the world

"world" a function involving a variable
a making required a given — the child
was given weather and a live oak profligate

of acorns. Own something small
is the advice I give.
When the Buddha walked on the earth

he left lotuses
as footprints.

Violets were sacred to Ares and Io.
The mother of Nichiren became pregnant
from dreaming of sun shining on a lotus.

Aleatory Agilities

How warm the weather how cold
the cause—the clever boys are playing;
against the odds the evening comes
upon them

maybe me, among the floral
appendages, down among the dreary
rooted dotted mint and bergamot some

kind of cage to live in, clouds above
and below clods to tread; a game
of remember the river, the boys
ride home

or I rode home, did, then, when
the visit was over, the cousins washing
the dishes now, talking about us
but we cross rivers returning

sleepy, restless, useless boys
time travellers all; into the future
at a rate to allow observation
in real-time;

the games begun the compass plant
and spiderwort trampled

there's no going back. Oh inconspicuous.
Oh me. The annals of Tacitus tell me
all I know of the age I live. In.
A storm is on the way.

~

The way a storm is, is inconceivable
collecting itself over time and landscape
then releasing a laughter of entropy,
energy as if
a question were asked. The answer involves
wind and water, always. And dust.
(In three dimensions there are five
regular solids; in four dimensions
six. A storm of disturbance.)

I am breathing in spite of the air
moving past me — but I cannot
not breathe and remain myself.
Is it I who breathe?

A storm in each lung, a disturbance
a havoc. *Crier havot.*

~

I asked him What do you
value most and his answer was,
Silence. Or, his answer was silence.
I cannot recall which.
I am aware that all things lie
hidden within clouds of things.
A storm is a cloud of things
and hides within itself a tumult
of time, times, brainlike. The boy
lingered too long in weather
watching the approach then
had to hurry home, chased
by the wind and various phased
waters — hail and rain and tears.

Marthe Reed

For myself as for writer David Malouf, the "real work of culture...[lies in] making accessible the richness of the world we are in, of bringing density to ordinary, day-to-day living in a place." Excerpted from a manuscript titled *the submerged land,* the poems articulate a language of place in which the burdens and the pleasures of this landscape move in dialogic tension: parallel recognitions of south Louisiana's beauty and its profound neglect. Networks of ancient cheniers, islands, and wetlands protecting the coast have been exchanged for oil-and-gas wealth. The Mississippi River has become a cipher inside its artificial embankments, a shipping lane and dumping ground, the ground waters in its reach poisoned by chemical factories. Yet each spring, live oaks spill their ovoid leaves, send out catkins, color every surface in chartreuse pollen, set acorns growing among their bright new leaves. Caspian Terns, Royal Terns, and Sooty Terns, Great Egrets and Reddish Egrets, Black Skimmers and Night Herons fish along the beaches and in the tangle of mangrove roots along the coast, nest in the boughs of cypress trees. The marshes, *les prairies tremblant,* glimmer greenly in the summer heat, sheltering fish, shrimp, and crab, nurseries of renewal. Drawn from the accumulation of particulars of living in south Louisiana over the past eleven years, a gradual sedimentation of experiences over time in *place,* the poems "[make] truth out of the multiple...a presence...come to the limits of language." (Alain Badiou) Engaging with the intertwining nodes of weather, culture, mineral exploitation, and geography that have resulted in a profoundly beautiful and productive landscape as well as a devastating reality in which every fifteen minutes an area of land the size of a football field is lost in Louisiana, the poems attend to that precipitous loss of land and its associated culture, homage to a vanishing realm.

Land and water (1)

> "No page is ever truly blank" – Craig Santos Perez, Saina

something else obtains
inexplicably

another luminosity
        (accretion   erosion)
between 2 bends in the Mississippi

a map or mapping
a loss a lost map
    the visible rend

white ibises   herons   egrets
Dow Chemical churning out polyethylene and methylcellulose

        ((milk jugs and
          milkshakes

wastestream emptying
((dioxin
into the Mississippi

vinyl chloride
a dead
((PVC
zone 1989 Morrisonville
cancer
alley

a "freetown" freed
((liberated
by Dow))
men and women bought out and
moved away   ((moved a
way

de-
populated by Dow
new town new
burial ground

Dow's sprawling 1,400 acre
grounds
PCBs   hexachlorobenzene   dioxin
produced in Louisiana and Texas
"confined to low-
            income African American communities"

disposal incinerators likewise
located
town wells poisoned
          (air
            poisoned)
abandoned

80 mile long
chemical corridor
Baton Rouge to New Orleans

a field aligned with

        supplication
        rushing water
        flight

any projected (pejorative) "field"   (of endeavor)
poisoned

    :: refinery   jobs a whole
      economy of exploitation

      between river and basin ((Atchafalaya
      (((Atchafalaya

      geography's bones   surfacing
      less and less
           steady

         this
           blank(ed) perspective (history's)
   page

coastlines

the sun   (((terra incognita

    glistens   water   ((terra nullius

          ((terra humida

      soaking
                air

lapse :: a city

       the city shifts on its piers   subsidence

                                                     inundation   :: a local
vernacular

     down-warping   alluvial earth   flood control and
navigational

              concerns chat like

     laughing gulls on

                           levees   lithosphere

                                  merely mud

          river's   ancient   deposition bird

                                          -foot shallow sea

   the weight of things   :: highways   bridges   rectilinear city

                sprawling toward water   coteau and

                                        yellow jack

        things of the past

                        sea rising over narrow shoals

                                                hydrology of

                                        channelization

                sun king's   flooded realm   le Conseil

        Souverain   erodes   brackish hem

                        :: salt grass and   wire grass

                                        lapse to fresh canouche

Billy Reynolds

I came of age in Huntsville, Alabama, in the late 1980s when the Huntsville Stars, the minor league baseball team, were the toast of the town, in large part due to Mark McGwire and Jose Canseco, a.k.a. "the Bash Brothers." I also grew up with a keen knowledge of the town's role in the history of U.S. space travel, so with the Challenger explosion still fresh in the town's collective memory, these "new" Stars were a big hit. But in writing the poem "Huntsville Stars," I wanted to erase these associations described above. "Huntsville Stars" is then my modest attempt to describe a place anew; it was my own strange good fortune to discover a story that took me beyond my limited field of vision.

ille Stars

at. Pond Beat. Spring Hill.
names gone to pasture when the land
was earmarked for the Redstone Arsenal.
And Elko Switch, the dirt road
to get you to each place with the little river
down below the moveable woods.

Back in the small and lost 1930s,
cotton fields and woody hollows,
trees blue with distance,
a woman, daughter of slaves,
who went by the name of Tessie,
was not picking someone else's cotton,

but watching the sky for clues,
an ever-darker sky, last frost,
and how neat the graves,
a brown cardinal darting among the leaves,
and the crickets consumed
with their own song, their own ways,

and a star falling in a far place.
Somewhere back there in hours
and weeks that make up time,
she measured grief with beads and string,
looking out the door at days of rain,
at the plain cheap pine box

in the room that was the same one
where she once dreamed of taking flight
where now her dead sister was laid out.
She rose and placed the home-strung necklace
on her sister, 33 black wire-wound beads,
Christ's age when he died,

and one blue glass bead in the center,
to ward off the evil spirits,
to duplicate the stars
which she thought of as children
of the sun or the eyes of the dead
watching far above a small dark field,

all the hands moving among the green.

jo reyes-boitel

My family history is framed by the place created by bodies of water, namely the Atlantic Ocean and the Gulf Coast. From my grandfather's childhood catching crabs on the beach to his desire to have his ashes placed in those same waters when he died. Before him, my grandmother's mother arrived in Cuba from Spain, traveling by boat alone as a young woman, to escape an abusive stepfather. Or after, when my mother visited Cuba thirty years after leaving and was given permission by a security guard to enjoy the public beaches that were meant only for tourists.

Everyday talk gives presence to the ocean and water: My daughter is a hurricane; my hips move like incoming waves; the humid wind in our central Texas city foretells the ocean's approach. Talk about the water is like talk about a crazy aunt, the one we all know, who lives free and holds family stories and raises hell. The ocean is an active participant in our family.

In recent months my work has moved toward the ocean as a carrier of people and ideas and challenges in all ways. I'm speaking specifically of the Middle Passage, where captured Africans were brought to the US and deposited along Texas' coastline. Each year a remembrance is given to those who landed on our shores, having survived the horrible journey, in order to honor the history that we can no longer access, the history within those souls. When I last attended the ceremony, it ended in our throwing multi-colored beans into the waves, asking for strength, support, blessings for our community, our family, our loved ones, our selves. The ocean is so large she carries it all.

Chan Chan

Oya: I've left my fingerprints at your cheeks   neck   shoulders

Hot and threatening sand beneath our feet
I close my eyes when you come toward me
I always close my eyes

Sun in our faces, this story is written somewhere
and the people watch us as an example of the ancient ways.

Why you are standing so far away?

It was a simple argument — Nothing compared to the struggle we witnessed when we were brought to this land. Nothing like what the entirety of the ocean witnessed through the passage. Yemaya, our mother, with her unblinking eye.

Our people lost in the water, others lost so quickly once on this land.

What of those on the islands between here and our homeland? Those who hung themselves on trees rather than be left without language and creation and family in exchange for our unwanted voyage?

What of those who live here now without connection to their ancestors? Their slippery feet unable to find root. Our children drifting further and further from us?

Enough already. You feel that tug. You know it's me calling you in from the flooded street.

Shake the root of me all you want. Call the lightning and charge the earth with all your anger if you must but return to me at once.

Return to me.

footnote to the romantic life

the unexpected glance [definition] :
1. a wind that is yet to arrive, even if an ocean smell already sits on your face
2. green water currents rushing against the walls of the eyes
3. two pairs of hands on a drum, when all the world decides to go quiet

see also: *now you've asked for it* and *my hem's come undone.*

Katherine Riegel

I've lived near Tampa, Florida for four years. Before that there was a stint in snowy upstate New York; before that it was all Midwest, birth to marriage. I have always written about the landscape of the Midwest, and probably always will. But here's the odd thing: the first poem I remember writing in college was an elaborate metaphor comparing the fields of the Midwest to the ocean. Now that I live near the Gulf, I understand that metaphor better. For me, the beach is about spaciousness, about huge skies and uninterrupted vistas and a sparseness of people. It is about peace, about the landscape being greater than we are and the comfort of that knowledge. I published my first book after I moved to Florida. I was lucky enough to be enfolded in the welcoming arms of the Southern literary community, and something about the land here keeps striking my heart—perhaps producing a different tone from the bells of Illinois, but something clear and inevitable anyway. Or maybe I just fell in love with the birds, those awkward cattle egrets in the fast food parking lot and the Florida population of sandhill cranes beside the mall. All I know is that the poems and I seem to find each other here, where everything from the spiders to the sunshine of December should be alien to me but instead beckons me onward like a roseate spoonbill stepping among the cypress.

And That Life

Beside the ocean I am not sure
whether I walk through sand or ashes.
Some magician threw my courage
into the air, where it became gulls
arcing and wheeling over a man spilling popcorn
on the dock around his feet. Some days
I just want to be the oyster living
under the weathered wood, clinging
to the pilings. I don't even care
whether I hold a pearl
or not. It would be simpler,
actually, to be free
of that irritant; to not have
to protect myself from the pain.
And that life: the flowering
open and closed with the tides. The water
running through me and coming out cleaner.

But no. Also the threat of the blade
slipped in and twisted, popping
me open to be devoured.

Acridophobia (Fear of Grasshoppers)

That first one
must have clamped its sharp feet
onto me like staples—

I felt fastened
to its alien chitinous body
rather than it to mine. I felt

it might carry me off
like a tender cookie
and eat me down to crumbs. How else

to explain my screams, then
and now, when those cigar-bodies
come close enough to

leer, carrying with them
the smell of sour kraut
and the relentless click-click-clicking

of a lighter that won't catch,
one of those long-nosed utility lighters
I desperately hold between myself

and them, wishing
I could burn them all down
to malevolent dust.

We Are Gulls

attacking the sea, diving into the surface
thinking our splash must be
magnificent. And who can tell what wonders
we find on the under side
where everything is slow and dim
and crackling with all
our other languages? Sometimes
we must run smack into it
to wake to another
consciousness. Sometimes we must dig
into the sand
before we can understand anything
about the stars,
anything about light at all.

Rena Rossner

I was born on Miami Beach, Florida, and my family vacationed in Naples, Sanibel Island and Key West—our favorite vacation spots. I lived two blocks from the ocean and could smell the sea breeze from my bedroom window which overlooked our backyard—planted with mango, avocado, orange and grapefruit trees. I spent my summers in marine biology and sailing camp amidst mangrove swamps, nurse sharks, stingrays, sand dollars and shells that line the Gulf shores. The sense of freedom and space, the flow of water, the sounds and scents and tastes of the sea and the rich landscape around me, the unique cuisine, the rhythms of latin music and the bright heat of the sun, years spent never owning anything other than open-toed shoes—that ethos is present in everything I write.

Aubaude with Citrus

The first night you were gone
barreling up to Scotland
I pictured rain, maybe it wasn't
really raining, the leaves
on the avocado tree outside
my door still shook. I watered it
with coffee grounds
from my cafetiere
like you taught me,
a fancy word. There was ozone
in the air, earth on my tongue, loss.
I plucked an unripe kumquat,
green and bitter,
rolled it in my palm,
saving the citrus scent for later,
when I'd need the smell
of hope on my hands, evidence.
A palmetto bug crossed my path,
I didn't crush it,
though the one that once crawled
under my sheets at midnight
still haunts my dreams. Some things
deserve to live.

Mary Jane Ryals

My blood was salted on the Gulf of Mexico, as both my parents were born in Daytona Beach in the early 1930s. My father's family members were shaggy pioneers in the early 1900s who settled in the forests, fished the fresh waters, killed wild hogs for food, and built their own yellow-pine house.

My mother remembers having to snuff out all lights on the Atlantic side during WW II when German subs cruised the coastline. I was raised knowing the sea was never more than an hour away by car.

Our family spent time on the Florida panhandle beaches from the time I was five. Deepest memories revolve around the flocks of wood storks, and white ibis and the blue-black grackles. I'd fall asleep on the porch of our makeshift beach house on Alligator Point to the hiss and sway of waves breaking shore.

My childhood was often spent underwater looking back up to surface waves. My sisters and I found bits of sea kelp, coral, sometimes dead sharks, always waves lapping to shore. We collected shells, bones, rocks, arrowheads, pottery over a thousand years old that the Gulf coughed up out of its shimmering monstrous body.

And now I'm feeling we are all separating from the land and water, watching civilization mine and ruin and disease all the things we find most dear on this Gulf. Yet there is no separation from ocean and us, family and ocean, birds and family, pottery and written language. So we write the place into us and flow it back out and back in and out again like a prayer of reminder, survival and hope.

After a Funeral at Cedar Key, Florida

– for Michael Trammell

We were eating. Ospreys were diving
near the graveyard. The sky was cold blue
by the cove on the bluff, and the sun was slanting
its winter gold, music's heat and hum.

Sun dove down the bluff. We
were relishing our lunch. The sky was slanting
its winter gold in the graveyard,
ospreys hungry and diving.

The sky was musical, hot and humming,
And the sun was slanting on the cove.
In the graveyard, music, hot and humming, dove
towards the sky, and we laughed,

rolling down the bluff towards the gulf.

Winter Beach Sighting

Walking in a red jacket on the beach,
The winter wind hurls across the sand,
And I see your face, Mother, at seven, dark
Brown hair, creamy fat cheeks, sunrise lips
and ocean. You carve a castle from grit.

But it's really my daughter, here on this
short Sunday afternoon, the brown Gulf
churning. Toes warm in the sand.

In your Florida, Mother, you watch
The Atlantic for flashing messages
in WW II code and German subs surfacing
off the coastline. The world went dark.
No lights, even at night, black curtains
in windows, no cigarettes in the cottages,
bitter salt of invasion on your lips.
I loved the big floppy hair bows
you wore in pink-tinted photos, that funny
front tooth overlapping the other. If I am
your mother now, I scoop you up, say,
*It's alright, darling. They'll never get us.
I know how this turns out.* Your hair
warm as a gull's feathers against my cheek.

A small wave scouring out my daughter's
sand castle brings me back. No bomb or hiding.
No darkness on her Gulf. No, don't be fooled.
Her war is keeping the lights on without oil.
Here, Mama, she says, handing me a stack
of horseshoe crab shells, translucent now
and briny. *Hold these.* A seven-year-old
command. She's willing to sacrifice nothing,
As if she can forecast what's ahead,
what she'll have to hold in her own hands.
What's behind her is her mother finding her
mother in her daughter. It's growing chilly
in the late afternoon rosy sunset.
I cover her with the red jacket.

What ocean does

Yesterday clouds tented gray over us
where we walked the gulf island, our brief away time
from the kids, the *swee-ash* of waves breaking land.
We spend so much time at home hating each other,
you said, an exaggerated joke you learned from me—
or I from you? It takes time to emerge
from the noise of children. Along the beach, shells
the color of peasant bread *shinked*
under our feet. Who else but us to blame
for the tedium of their need? Purple
everywhere, violet stripes on shell,
lavender atop the dune, lilac shadow
of water-soaked sand. *No, you cook dinner.*
Look, you're spoiling the kids again. I'm so tired.
This black and blue dissolves with midday.
Who knows what heals in the absence of pull
big as the world. The ocean salted my skin,
taste of human sweat. *It's chilly for short sleeves,*
you said. These sounds, music of our essence,
dissonant and melodic—How else could life
make its noise? Sun's rays slanted back at land,
burned through clouds. *Look, a sun hole,* I said.
A holy moment, you said, your unintended pun
saturated with the *shink* and *swee-ash* in you.

Danielle Sellers

I grew up in Key West, Florida. Behind our home was a deep canal which led into a bay in the Gulf of Mexico. For me, home and this body of water are one in the same. The water factored into nearly everything we did. If it wasn't the vehicle for a family outing, it was the background. My childhood was spent in it, on it, and surrounded by it. For a time, we owned a houseboat and my extended family would take overnight trips almost every weekend. There was nothing better than sleeping in the hot backcountry air, hearing the water lap against the boat. The Gulf was a thing I loved and feared. I loved it because my father loved it. He was a great fisherman, and when we were out on the water he was calm and happy. I feared the sharks he brought out of it. I feared the unknown. As a teenager, my friends had boats and we'd have keg parties on the sandbars. That was my normal. I've lived far from the Gulf for fifteen years now and its absence in my everyday life is like a kind of death. I feel it like I feel the absence of many family members, now dead. When I smell the seaweed and salt air, it signals not only a return home, but a return to myself.

Friendship Bracelet

for Claire

Landlocked in northern Mississippi,
my friend revives the middle school art
of friendship bracelets. Twined in mine
are the colors of the sea. She knew
to weave for me the one thing I miss daily.

To be without it is a loss felt constantly,
like a dull ache under the scapula—
not important enough to mention
in those lists of grievances we give friends.

~

The clear water we lived in
on the weekends, after school,
or reaching the pinnacle of a bridge,
saw miles of every day and still,
even to a native, it took the breath.

~

In the shallows,
long rows

of sand
furrowed,

the current
a machine.

~

There are always more
flotillas of seaweed piling in.
That sour, aging father smell
only a daughter can love.
Breathing it in, breathing it out,
a kind of cleanse, a return.

~

The worst is not knowing.

Over clear water, a shadow
could be cloud, could be shark.

But we do it anyway, plunge in.

If I Died Now,

he would drive to Mississippi, fetch you
down the spine of Florida to the island

we first loved, where our ancestors
settled and burgeoned like sponges,

where I broke myself against coral and limestone
so many times I left for fear of drying up.

You'll be hers, this Cuban woman who paints,
silver earrings flashing under her boundless hair.

As girls together, we were often asked
if we were sisters, my face one shade lighter.

I was wild, but she was wilder
in tie-dyed dresses and Keno sandals.

She communed with the dead,
smoked grass, speared groupers.

She couldn't wait to be a mother, and didn't.
She's given you brothers and sisters.

I have spent too much time wishing her ill
these last years, afraid she'd win you too.

You'd treasure her like a mother,
and your father would never mention my name.

December Evening, Key West

Today I sat on the seawall behind the house
I've lived in twenty years, watching mullet
turn circles in the canal. Impossible
to count how many, it always looks like more
spiraling in from the unprotected bay.
They raise their silver bellies to the sun,
flashing like strobe-lights under water.
Some thing unseen hunts them,
most likely barracuda. Occasionally one
or a few leaps from the edge to the hub.
The ripple rings expand and disappear.
The school, a gilded body, burrows
three feet, its lights subdue, shapes
distort. On a whim one brave or stupid fish
pilots them back. They form a plane,
then vortex, octagon, what could be
a shield. We sold this place last week.
I thought of the mullet swimming the still canal,
and wondered how they never tired
of turning their bellies to the sun,
or understood how close I came to jumping in.

Martha Serpas

I was born in the second-largest Cajun settlement in Louisiana. My friends from anywhere else say our Main Street is a bayou lined with trawlers. We have crawfish boils on Fridays in Lent: Cajun Catholicism is a mutual inculturation. You've heard about the hospitality. It's the place to get lost, get a flat, or decide to just drop by. There's a corresponding clannishness. Being born thirty miles away can make you a Texían, nonnative.

I was six months in the womb when Betsy hit. Like Augustine or Malcolm X, I consider the wails and cracks that I heard and felt in the uterine undertow the beginning of my theological upbringing. I get confused about the approximate dates of crawfish season, shrimp season, oyster season—good food just shows up—but hurricane season runs June 1 to November 30. That I never forget.

Everything I know, or want to know, about this life I understand through the marsh—its variations of green, the solid water, solitary ghost trees that won't grow and won't fall down. Binaries subside and are built up. Nothing seems to move, but the swamp is a shimmering paradox. The land in the Barataria-Terrebonne Estuary is disappearing faster than any other on Earth. I write elegies even as I work for its preservation. Some new life takes the place of what dies—we all know that—but it pains me that I can't see the bit of life that will come next.

Yet more houses are built, and there are no for sale signs.

And, of course, all of this milieu and mystery exists because 1,000 years ago my bayou, Bayou Lafourche, was the Mississippi River and built my home from scooped-up mud on its way to the delta. All of me exists because of the Gulf.

Betsy

Without my vigil, it happens. Bright green fern,
      humeral veil of ordinary time,

covers these crossed oak branches as if
      the sky is too holy for wood to touch.

In the dry days before, I admire
      the cracked bark and dark brown color

of my eyes and hair, the resistance
      I lack, the wisdom the wind brings every

hurricane season. September 9th,
      1965, I waited like a reef

in my mother's womb, listening to small
      branches crack and rain land insistent

against the drumming clapboard, a bedroom
      window finally giving in. I could breathe

the rising water, fire ants, a used-up
      black moccasin less patient

with the erratic tide than I.
      The only levee between me and

the known seething world was flesh and regret,
      and beyond, the silver wash hiding

the familiar. Men would come much later,
      sinking their shoulders and shovels

into the soft land, the uninhibited water.
      And because the mud peels open for them,

they think they have won. Their high places become
      low places again. Single-minded. Graceful.

God, how I want to tell you this story!
    The plywood goes up from inside,

as it must, nailed to the frame, the wind banned
    from what's left of the house, and everyone

exhales and shakes their wet clothes, except me
    who's been drenched and naked, carefree,

for months in the uterine undertow,
    or maybe beyond months, belonging to

a steady thought (not mine) that repeats itself,
    one that won't translate to resurrection.

Conversion

The tracks got ripped up like a busted zipper,
thrown down, piles of tar and broken ties,
into the dead grass on the bayouside.

You have to understand: only time tears things
down here. Long after you quit a house, pack
up and leave, that house stands

Catalogued, under sheets of rust, paneless,
porchless, for years. Cast-iron kettles
won't move, won't be moved,

The air above their bellies, still and sharp.
No one remembers the cane they boiled
or how they came to kill grass

Where they do. Half an old bridge
makes a sweet fishing spot—but taking
the rails away, it was an insult, really,

A theft. I saw how one loss collapses
into another, the rings between them,
almost indistinguishable.

But then, to the right of the road,
the shoulder leapt with sunflowers,
the blue sky dangled like a scarf,

And the part of me that was buried
came back like the dead after hard rain,
just pushed up the glass lid

And stepped onto solid ground. Backwater rises
to its own schedule, covers the highways,
you can't tell the bayou's banks

From the road's edge, and then there's no question
of staving off conversion.
Even the dead won't be held down.

The Water

In the morning the water waits like a deckhand,
a persistent curl against the shore,

who won't back down, take no, or be denied.
It is there under the wharf and soon under

the house, whoring with any swamp rat
or snake. It rings cypress knees with pearls—

it dreams under the sun like cut cane,
throwing back the salt you wash away,

then wearing pilings down to air.
Your houses wade on stilts tall as pillars,

their sheet-metal skulls bared to a mildewed
sky. Against the fallen trees rain and lapping

tide meet, slapping of nets and fish and
naked children pulling driftwood boats

in one joyful noise around your sleep.
In the afternoon the water is there, only more,

browner and grayer, no sweeping seaweed or foam,
just its presence farther up your shore,

like a dull brother-in-law in front of TV.
He means something to somebody—

but not you, not just now. Its slow wake seems
harmless, the litany of waves before a storm

rolling benignly ashore. Intoxicating!
And then it is there, all gray length of it,

rich sex of it, it wants you so badly,
it pounds at the door, *Let me take*

*your smallness, your jetties, your broad
coasts, your loam.* It gathers

at night beyond the curtain of mosquitoes,
darker than the shut-down sky,

the boarded-up clouds. Its desire
thrums like an idling outboard. Ignore

it, and it tows itself into your dreams. It's
everywhere, every chance, all the time.

It is more certain than death or love.
It must have been conceived by death and love.

When the last silt sinks under your feet,
you will have to walk out on this water.

Paul Siegell

Goose somehow got me to overcome my fear of oysters, and now oysters are the most delicious. Better than mussels. Slurp. For the past 14 years, "Thanksgiving" has meant a flight from either Pennsylvania or Georgia to family and Ft. Myers Island Beach, my happy body flopping in the gentle Gulf. Blackened Grouper. Predatory Pelicans. Headline through our Camp Coleman circle of friends: "Body found in Mississippi Sound identified as missing Georgia man Samuel Begner." Found "by a man checking on crab pots." When I was about to leave for Guatemala, an editor-friend told me he was in some store at a mall in Alabama years ago and overheard an old couple talking about the "MADE IN" tag that was on some item they were looking at and the man goes, "Since when did they start making these things in Guatem, Alabama?" When we went from 1999 to 2000, I, along with 75,000+ others, was dancing on a field at the Big Cypress Seminole Indian Reservation of the Everglades. Alligators still alive in the A.M. Nine of us packed into some small double-bed hotel room a few blocks from Bourbon Street. I took the floor next to the radiator. Around 4 in the morning, "E" in a bed with "S" woke us up crying for "J" to help him with the puke that "S" just unconsciously introduced into the night of hells yes Jazz Fest red beans and rice. Hours later in the sun-shot room, I awoke to "S" whining out in her most adorable, "Why isn't anyone sleeping with me?" We're gonna need more towels.

05.04.07 – New Orleans Jazz Vipers – Spotted Cat, NOLA

— for Stanley the Cab Driver (not the ghost)

pulsed/impaired, fleur-de-lis zombies
brush-stroked with eyes over their bags under their eyes,
feel out past their frames
in a bar on Frenchmen Street;
and from the walls they're
hung upon,
they watch over all the mud-bug madness
of an un-amp'd/amp'd seven-piece swing band, plus special
guest Washboard Chaz, like circumstantial "FOR SALE" signs—

for the Spotted Cat's flooded
with *Abita* Amber-ordering, just-flew-in-from-where evers
for the happy JazzFest weekend, but

another kind of Kat, one not of notes, but of the stricken
Crescent, has indeed painted its
own cold strokes of colorless woe
clear across too many lives and too many Creole cottages
too many feet high up the walls.

a Cajun two-step, a Zydeco strut,
a "MAKE LEVEES, NOT WAR" bumper sticker.

stylish iris, flower a-the lily, crawfish of the fleur-de-lis:

havoc carcass toxic "2 dogs dead" of devastated
fleur-de-lys in the attic
in the Super Dome on wrought-iron balconies; alas:

fleur-de-lis as tear, but with tail feathers still shakin' true—

po boy fleur-de-lis saints
acoustic-bass bass-sax sax fiddle trumpet clarinet and
acoustic guitar fleur-de-lis festivities—

crawfish a-crawlin', *this town's so cool even the trees wear beads!*

05.05.07 – Jonathan Freilich, Skerik, Stanton Moore, Todd Sickafoose & Mike Dillon – Chickie Wah Wah, NOLA

like percussive
        puppeteers, when

                drumsticks/when vibraphone
              mallets friendly-fire strike/whack
             /collide with their skins
           and metal bars—some
          idea of my body/some
         flesh to express a feel,
        moves. fond of funk,
       jazzed to jam, *I'm the*
      guy in the moon man
     boom box t, and it's a
    pleasure to react ecstatic
   to such fusion of N'awlins
  cuisine. "Unless you feel it
 emotionally," Chickie Wah
Wah's owner said, hand-to-
forehead then brushed over
scalp, "you can't understand."
 shadow of how fast a pedal-
  breathing, metallic xylo-like
  vibraphone a-bullion treasure
  bars, Dillon up—tips of Sick-
  afoose acoustic bass: thump
 thu-thump ah thump-thump,   *thwong—*
 coins of black sax pad-cups   smooth sailing
 thru Skerik vending machine   of sweet jazz-kitchen
 delights—tongue of "NAKED" Freilich out for charged
  guitar face & author of songbook open on tambourine—
  all playing with and against one another somewhere
   within the transparent fan of trails created by he
    who speaks in strikes of sticks—*gimme*
     some Moore! gimme that whomp of
      full moon bass kick and tap
        dance a-the

tightest spiders on my eardrums—

for while an old friend who flew into NOLA from L.A.
to be with girl who flew into NOLA from N.Y.
leaves the show early to go get laid, I've come
to N'awlins *for* New Orleans.

ire'ne lara silva

Until I was eighteen, I followed my parents who worked as migrant farmworkers/truckdrivers. We followed the harvest seasons of different crops from South Texas to varying points on the map over time—Mathis, Bay City, Oklahoma, Dalhart, Turkey (Texas), Hereford, Dimmit, New Mexico—and then back to South Texas. No matter how much or how little time we spent there, South Texas (the Rio Grande Valley) was our home. The appearance of palm trees along the highway as we returned always thrilled me. Throughout my childhood and after I returned after college, South Padre Island or the Port of Brownsville was only a thought and a short car trip away. The Gulf of Mexico fed me—fed my eyes and fed my language and fed my memory. Its vastness. Its freedom. The unceasing waves. The wind. What little regard it had for what maps said it was or who it belonged to.

The Gulf of Mexico as well as South Texas as well as the border are everywhere in my writing. How we are restricted and how we are boundless. How we are defined and how we are infinite.

I may not live there anymore—though from Austin, the Gulf is still only a thought and a (slightly longer) car trip away—but that is always the place I will name as my home. Where one country meets the other. Where the earth meets the ocean.

tierra

there are days when   i   wake
with the taste of   tierra in my mouth
                        i
            eat and taste tierra
            speak and taste tierra
it has gone deep in me
        i can smell it on my skin   like the earth
before rain   i
      taste salt and green things on the
tip   of my tongue   in every word
everything   i   eat has the edge
        of earth in my mouth   a grittiness of sand
against my teeth   i   feel caracoles and roots
crystals and leaves   blood on my tongue
        i
              taste tierra when
i look at the sky
        when   i take a step the earth
swallows me   i have swallowed it
i taste it   it tastes me every time
              i   breathe it in
esta tierra es tuya   yo soy de la tierra
maíz tastes like tierra   y sal y sudor and my blood in
my veins tastes like tierra
           to my flesh your mouth tastes
like tierra   i
drown in zoquete   grow roots into your flesh
         i
            swallow salt from your skin
    know you are part of the earth part of me
but not mine   i am not yours
       we belong to the tierra
    esta tierra es mía yo soy de la tierra
                    tierra
that birthed me
darkened me   fed me
        cradles me still

diabeticepidemic

la azucar we heard it whispered first
la azucar they said but it made no sense
the sugar the sugar she died from *la azucar*
at first it was only the old people
the only difference we saw
was that coffee needed sweet n low instead of sugar
and maybe they'd eat only half a piece of *pan dulce*
instead of two

and then it was my father
i was ten he seemed the same
nothing we could see was different
though every morning he pulled out a vial
from the refrigerator and gave himself a shot
they told him he had to eat differently
but didn't tell him why or how to eat the food
in the little guidebook
half of which he'd never seen before

and there were stories but those were about other people
years passed and then it was everyone's grandparents
and some aunts and uncles though they were all at least fifty years
old
we heard of children who had it but only saw them on tv with
jane fonda while on mexican tv there were all these commercials
that
said
this pill this plant this doctor can make you better

la azucar was everywhere
but not as scary as cancer cancer would kill you
i went to college and learned nothing at all about it
and then returned to south texas
where the people are ninety eight percent
hispanic latino mexican tejano whatever name they like most
and by this time people could say *la azucar*
and everyone understood
not to insist not another tortilla no more cake no beer
and there was splenda and diet coke and sugar free snow cones
in every restaurant and on every corner

everything changed when it was my brother my youngest brother
in the hospital for gallstones though it took two weeks, six e.r. visits
and two hospital admittances before they operated
and it was on the third or fourth visit when they asked
you know you're diabetic?
and said *oh and you have high blood pressure and high cholesterol
and are you a pima indian I've read studies many pima indians
have all three diabetes high blood pressure and high cholesterol*

everything i learned from my brother i shared
with anyone who asked anyone who confided in me
how many people on the verge of tears who didn't understand why
old people young people thin people round people white people brown
people
everyone says type two diabetes can be controlled with diet and exercise they lay all the blame on obesity but not every body is the same
there are all kinds of factors all kinds of resistances
and the right medication for one person is wrong for another

i changed my diet gave up drinking
thought i'd managed not to become a target
no one told me not sleeping and skipping meals and stress
and living on adrenaline could tear the body down
or that insulin resistance was part of poly-cystic ovarian syndrome
and then that day came the confirmation from the doctor
and my first shot of insulin and now *la azucar* was in my body
part of my life and it was a while
before i could see anything outside myself
without my brother i think i would have given up given in

it took awhile but then i opened my eyes
and noticed that *la azucar* was all around me
the woman next to me at work
the early morning bus driver
every third person at my other job
and the man at the store puzzling over egg substitutes
and the waitress downing a shot of orange juice during a long shift
and everywhere i see the warning signs in people's behaviors
in their complaints symptoms beyond passing
thirst or temporary blood sugar lows
but no one listens

why isn't there screaming in the streets
the children are diabetic the pregnant women are diabetic
so many people of color so many poor and working class
and the food is making us sick
and every day there are more and more of us
and *la azucar* is claiming lives and limbs and whole families
why is *la azucar* still being whispered
we should be screaming it

Jay Snodgrass

I have always tried to escape to the sea. I live in Tallahassee, Florida, and Apalachicola has become for me the new southernmost point I can resort to when I feel the urge to return to what submerged voice calls me from the depths.

Apalachicola

So much is rotten by the sea, pits
of the mollusk, mounds of shell
beneath a cotton of seagulls.
The scent is a wallop of sea bed,
regurgitated round husk of rock stomach
beside the restaurant's gullet.

A diving helmet reflects
the parade of tourists.
Cats weave handouts from the benzene
parking lot. So much plight,
a bobbing carcass of mullet
in the march grass.

A veteran fishes from the pier,
harassing girls for sport. Crease
of sunlight in his forehead
nicotine and fish stain, nictitating
eyelid, a gaze predatory and hollow,
he hands out lollipops to little girls.

There is a bridge and a bank
and not much else of pride.
The sea-wash etches calligraphy
into the seawall, barnacle
punctuated. Beneath this line
oysters bed the difference.

Andrea Spofford

I believe that place is an integral part of how I define myself, and as a result my writing frequently addresses place in a very explicit way. Spending a significant time on the coast of Texas during my childhood, and now living in southern Mississippi, it is difficult for me to separate the Gulf from my experiences of place. In my writing I attempt to locate myself within geographical experience and emphasize the larger impact of environmental concerns. I want to show that geographies affect everyone, demonstrating how we are not isolated by our personal environmental experiences. The paradox is that "place" seems local and specific but can in fact build bridges and unite us in global, potentially universal, ways. Though each of my poems focuses on different aspects of environment and identity, what I think best describes my writing is found in the intersection of person and physical place—just as I exist as a product of my physical location, so too does everyone else.

(Oncorhynchus mykiss)

Trout's belly slick twisted so smooth
and wet your tongue
fog your mouth against my ear
like fingertips freezing red to purple
numbed snow and sparking fire
we should tingle in cold air, burn later
naked in snow we are nothing—
slick fish twisting through water, sharp finned, horrific.

Victoria, Texas

I.
This spring in Texas in the outskirts of town the wind is so harsh the sky is so white the girls in bright purple dresses drift across the hillside above the river like blossoms blown from trees the shades changing in the sun and shadows.

II.
This spring in Texas the Guadalupe River is swollen and green oak trees swim upon submerged banks flanking pathways of sinking red brick staircases tumbling into thick heavy water churned up and up by wind and current swirling leaves reflecting white skies.

III.
This spring in Texas we drive at eight over bridges and roads that quake and bend blind hills and curves over tall grasses a wild turkey in the field feathers upright against the wind the sky quickening dark blue to heady drops of rain down and down upon seven girls in purple dresses spinning into storm clouds.

Sheryl St Germain

My childhood home is located three blocks from Lake Pontchartrain and one mile from the Mississippi, both of which find their way to the Gulf of Mexico. As a child I spent summers on the barrier island of Grand Isle in the Gulf with my family, and later fell in love with the Atchafalaya Basin, a river delta area where the Atchafalaya River and Gulf of Mexico merge. My voice, character, and imagination have been indelibly shaped by these waters. I learned that what was beautiful could also turn deadly in a hurricane; and I learned to live comfortably in an ambiguous landscape where what was land could easily become water and vice versa. I learned that waters that were polluted could still provide a space for reflection to feed my developing imagination. It is not an exaggeration to say I learned poetry through an intimacy with these waters.

For many years I have been concerned about the loss of cypress trees as well as the ability to make a living, as Cajuns traditionally did, fishing in the Atchafalaya Basin. Unrestricted logging from the past and unsustainable practices with respect to the way we build levees and manage water, are causing a region of almost unfathomable natural riches to suffer in equally unfathomable ways; "Crossing the Atchafalaya" is a lament for the damage we are causing.

Pontchartrain

> —For the first time since the BP oil spill began, oil reached
> Lake Pontchartrain Monday in the form of tiny tarballs.
> - *Eyewitness News*, July 10, 2010

no other lake has this slate-blue color
solemn, almost, as if the lake knows
how important it is, this blue with

more than a hint of gray, almost
the color of my hair is these days, this blue
I walked to every day in the summer,

this blue with more than a hint of gray
where a boy, lost in the last hurricane
once asked me to marry him, this blue

where our family ate fried seafood on Friday nights
at restaurants that used to jut out on piers
that smelled like shrimp and creosote and beer,

this blue with more than a hint of gray in whose polluted
waters I swam and skied and fished with brothers
who loved this wounded blue

like a god, this blue that pierces me now
with its smell of crabs and fish and salt,
this blue I look out at today after all

the boats and bikes and restaurants
have hurricaned to its bottom, this blue
resting place

for boyfriends and brothers
and countless others who faces swirl
in the blue, the gray, the tar.

Crossing the Atchafalaya

—for Greg Guirard

1
our boat cuts through muddy water to black,
water with oxygen to water without
and back again, winding around giant stumps
of old growth cypress, all that's left
from when this swamp was logged to almost
nothing a hundred years ago

if you close your eyes you can imagine them:
thousands upon thousands of living trees
thousands of years old, mute shades
that ghost this almost empty stretch of water

the air would have smelled like cypress then
and the other gone ones—ivory billed woodpeckers—
would have thrived in those thick trunks
that would have risen twenty-five times
taller than us into the heavens

their lime green leaves
would have ceilinged the sky

2
bald cypress lives long but grows slowly

the small trees that dot the Basin now
might be a hundred years old, not yet
mature, though big enough,
some say, for garden mulch

3
still there's life here: crawfish burrow
in water around cypress knees, ospreys build nests
on top of dead trees, woodpeckers drum,
barred owls nest in tree cavities,
herons, egrets and Cajuns fish the tea-brown water,
bear and deer, possum and bobcat

fox, coyote and armadillo hunt the edges,
beavers and otter, snakes slither everywhere

there's a giant alligator nearby,
Greg says, but we only look halfheartedly for it —
we've seen many over the years, and some things
are better left alone

4
the swamp is hemmed in with levees,
bayous are damned and the river can't move
like it once did, so some days the water goes black
and kills everything caught in it

Greg's crawfish traps are almost empty with the dead today —
we boat from trap to trap, *black water,* he says
as he pulls up trap after trap of dead ones
no air in the water

5
we know what else lies under these waters:
massive trunks of ancient cypress
                    honey-yellow and auburn,
thick as three alligator bodies, trees felled
from a time when loggers took
everything, and if one fell into the water,
well there was enough to waste

just a few of the great giants still stand
in a secret place you can find if you ask

we visit them at sundown after the day
of dead crawfish, the waters bloody
from the sinking sun, Spanish moss
silver and hopeful on the limbs of the few trees
that are left: guardians of a rich graveyard —

their song haunts me to bone

Sunnylyn Thibodeaux

The poet Kevin Opstedal once referred to me as a "New Orleans poet stranded in San Francisco." Some identities we just can't shake. I grew up two blocks off the levee to the Mississippi River with the seasonal excitement of hurricanes. We never evacuated. My parents didn't ever flinch at boarding up and hunkering down, so I learned early of the romantic side of humidity and gale force winds. And those early life lessons, being one with the powerful force of nature as she roars, are where and when the young artist thrives and develops. Now, I live surrounded by different waters, with a different excitement of nature at her best. But what will always find its way into my work is the South: the waters, the thickness of the air, the Yat'isms.

I was pregnant and home for a visit at the time of the Gulf oil spill which was like pulling the rug out from under someone gaining their strength to walk. It was beyond heartbreaking, more frustrating maybe. The disaster found its way into my work much quicker than I had thought. Katrina had taken me almost two years to let into the work, and it wasn't necessarily by choice. The poem wants what it wants when it knows you're ready to be tapped as a source portal. Then ULL student Mickey Shunick went missing this summer and that snuck into the poem too. I dig my heels in firmly on being a NOLA girl, quite proud to represent the bayou and the bends and all the mates in between with poetry. It's a characterization I never intend to strip, not on the page or in the self.

Evangeline, How Do You Call Your Tribe

— for Mickey Shunick

Down at the bayou the summer beamed on
        no matter what news got my gut to pit
Small college town overgrown with haunts
           of bodies tossed to swamp. Drowning
              in chatter. A good year for hunting
    I peddled the streets named for presidents and saints
past the halls I pulled all my hair out in. Bike in the basin
Two fishermen spot black and gold. Late night surveillance
down to St. Landry   Charred out truck over the state line
    What gets replayed in the head – sorted past, unregistered status
                  Ties to the year I left
        Swamp deep bellow, rhythm of rain
It's not that I am. It's not like I know.
I could. I don't. I could be.
            Thirteen year lapse, not a likely drift
          Frayed angels down the line
     Bargained out disclosure, behind Claire Point
        The hunt for a swamp iris
            for a moment never quite right
                rattled by a system
      We don't dare breathe
      We don't dare beckon
Between the flicker of light and the stars
This is the way back home

Not Quite Colorado Bound

Do you remember the whisper green
       air, light creeping
             up your forearm
                     to touch your shoulder

We left on a day when the devil was beating his wife
How summer often goes. You said,
you were cold but everything was lit otherwise.   Over   mountains
               down to river beds, palms fiving warm air,
catching
flies. We drove for days and days
         sleeping in rain, belting out
             repetitives as if melodies. We tripped out
               on all the rustles and silence, flickers and fades

Looking out for rattlers and bears, we forget
               what's in people. No one could take us
        No one was there   Fourteen years
went
        Altitude adjustments, less is
            lost from the ground,
from
               the canyon. *Wandering*
        Star was one of them. The night
     shedding its mystery
   as we headed back south
All things go
All things do go

Jay Udall

After living in the American West for nearly twenty years, I moved with my wife and daughter to south Louisiana in the summer of 2011 to take a teaching job. We've found great beauty here—in the brilliant music, in the mix of cultures, in the wildlife. The birds alone—bald eagles, herons, egrets, ibis, anhingas, roseate spoonbills, to name just a few—are stunning.

Yet there's also extensive degradation of the land and water, due to the careless practices of the petroleum and agricultural industries. The human cost is evident. Health care professionals have dubbed the part of the state below Baton Rouge "cancer alley," but this title doesn't do full justice to the range and frequency of immunodeficiency disorders that plague this area.

Recently, because Louisiana is losing landmass at an astonishing rate—a football field's worth every forty-five minutes—people have begun to think more closely about their relationship to this place. Yet there's a long, long way to go before a sustainable balance is struck between use and preservation.

In my poems I'm trying to imagine my way into this place through the honoring of its particulars. To pay attention is to value, and to argue for the greater life-web that sustains our being.

Louisiana 1 South in Winter

Drive down through Lockport and Larose,
through Cut Off and Golden Meadow,
past the signs offering live crab and crawfish,
past the shrinking towns and moldering shacks,

and the margins come to meet you —
silted water reaching up
to both sides of the two-lane,
the dulled green land scattering

into patches that seem to float
like you now, detaching
from memory — surfaces
you touch lightly passing over

as power lines step to a slow drowning,
houses lift over you on stilts,
and bridges arc in vague promises
of more than water and sky.

At road's end you arrive in Grand Isle,
not so grand, the Gulf in February gray
gnawing the shore. Here life feels storm-beaten,
clinging like the few live oaks left,

dwarfed and brittle as the seashells
shattering underfoot while you tread the edge
of what cancels and returns your eyes,
vast monotony through which summer

hurricanes gather themselves and come.
Someone in you soon turns to
go while there's still a way back.
Someone stays, staring out.

'madillo

        I can't count
      a promise
never made, sometimes kept

when you surreptitiously
tiptoe down summer night
streets between, under

parked cars, through ditches
and culverts, behind bush
and brush, with that head

you might have stolen from
some newborn kangaroo,
long ears like curled leaves,

tapered snout that sees
for feeble eyes any
ant or beetle, any

subterranean grub
or root, any tossed
scrap of fruit or half-

eaten hamburger
waiting in a wrapper.

In hard light I've seen
on roadsides that same armor
crushed by rushing steel tons,

corpses so common they blind
us to your prehistoric
glory, your nine plates

gates into another
story of the body
in the book of Earth,

your untamed flame venturing
through the large darkness,

   returning the night.

Jerry Wemple

I lived in Southwest Florida for six and a half years. The move came abruptly. My mother and new stepfather had "won" a trip to Lehigh Acres. Such prizes were common marketing schemes. Though they did not buy in Lehigh, we moved south just before Christmas 1969.

While officially part of Cape Coral, my neighborhood – two half-mile-long cul-de-sacs, one paved, one not – was a remnant of nearby North Fort Myers. Cape Coral is a 120 square mile pre-planned community cut from mangroves and palmettos. Most of its population lay to the south, living in air conditioned houses with screened pools and patios, the houses sitting on lush sodded and landscaped lots. At the end of our short street, an old man grew a plot of sugar cane. Most of the houses were small and needed repairs. Some were actually trailers with plywood additions.

It took some time to adjust to Florida, but after a while I came to love land. Or rather, I came to love the water. I spent as much time as I could on the water, often hooking school to go jump off the Blind Pass Bridge linking Sanibel and Captiva islands. Depending of the tide, you could ride the warm current hundreds of yards into the shallow bay, or if you weren't careful, hundreds of yards out into the Gulf of Mexico. Sometimes I'd go swimming in the nearby freshwater canals, more wary of water moccasins than the alligators swimming nearby. By the time I was sixteen, I figured I wanted to work for the Lee County Sheriff's Department, maybe skipper an airboat as part of a marine patrol. But one summer my mother decided she'd had enough of my alcoholic stepfather, and just like that we moved back north.

Half a Mile Off Everglades City, Florida

The water is shallow here.
A good-sized man,
finding himself and his boat
tipped over, could stand
and walk to the mangrove shore.
No gators in the salt to bother
you, but don't do it
on the inside of the bay
where sets of floating eyes
scour the surface
looking for a mistake.

The water is shallow here,
and warm as a bath. Piss-warm,
warm as a can of beer left out
in the afternoon sun.
March winds don't reach
down this far. No one
has to say it:
This is as far as you can go
and remain unchanged.

The water is shallow,
yet big fish swim in it.
Fish big as a hog.
Big as those tawny,
one-hump cows standing
in the pine-dotted pastures
a mile inland. Those lonesome
cows forced to keep
tick-eating snow-white egrets
as companions.

The water the color of a faded emerald.
The Park Service tourist boat
cuts through it as the engine spits.
The smell of brine and mildewed
life preservers drips down
the back of your throat
like uncut cocaine.

A pelican dives and finds his dinner
in it. Translucent shrimp tickle
the inside of his pouch. A cormorant,
black as the Big Cypress Swamp at midnight,
finds a perch and spreads his wings to dry.
Over a crackling speaker, a sun-bleached
guide, dressed in the standard — khaki shirt
and faded jeans — drones on.

The water is shallow here.
And pure and clear.
Eight miles out it touches the sky.
The sky is so clear
that it may be possible
to look right past Mexico,
all the way around the world,
and see the Holy St. John
dipping Jesus into deep blue
waters of the River Jordan.

Patti White

This is where they will scatter my ashes: in a back channel of Lemon Bay. Past the grass flats and oyster beds, south of Angler's Resort, a bit north of the narrow mouth of Stump Pass. In water shaded by masses of mangrove and seagrape, guarded by broken pines. Just there: in a shallow stretch of purest aquamarine.

To the east, beyond a puzzle of islands, a small town; to the west, across the key, the glory of the gulf. It is a very short walk to the small and intimate waves. You can watch the sun boil the horizon before you turn back to the bay, and with your dazzled eyes you will see me, a red and white bobber on the surface of the water. Adrift at the end of an invisible line.

Sarasota

Alabaster clouds crumble like sugar cubes
blessed with rum, grains melted on a tongue
curled around a pleasing sweetness. Silk
drifts onto the veranda, a veil of sheer
eggshell rainfall spattering Saint Elmo's
fire on a fan blade's nickel wing. Sea oats
gain purchase on the dunes, and great blue
herons crowd the canal, stick legs stalking
igneous mussels in the milky mangrove silt.
Jacaranda blossoms tremble in the wind, as if
Krakatoa had erupted, ashen, far away, and
low waves of loss had circled the earth.
Marbled lightning leaves a trace of sharp
nicotine in the humid air, a train bound for
Opelika rumbles its bauxite boxcars as it
passes mournful glades and marshes,
quiet towns half-dead from heat and
raddled with desire, acres of palmettos,
slow cane fields blazing before dark.
Tremors and faults crack a glassine world
under a grass-blown sky of porcelain,
velocity a trauma that sends us weeping,
warbling like robins in the Cuban laurel, small
xenophobes clinging to waving branches,
yellow eyes alight with anxiety, tiny hearts like
zinc-lined sinks, shiny bright, full of water.

Bovine

The doorman, blue uniform, gold-braided hat, a bank of elevators, all open. Delicate scratches on the malachite floor. A smudge or smear. A wet swipe and swirl, a hint of warm breath. A mist on the silvered door. A character traced, a scoop and scallop. Buttons cracked: floor twelve, floor seven. Buttons flashing uncanny amber. Floors above floors and more floors. A terrace garden, potted oregano ravished, a tall palm overturned. At the end of a long hall, a broken window. A breeze blowing in. A faint smell of hay blowing in. Broken glass on the carpet. A breeze, a wisp of hay. A glass of buttermilk on a table, a tumbler of buttermilk on a table on the terrace. A white linen tablecloth beneath the glass. A breeze blowing the palm fronds, the tablecloth, a forgotten pot of lavender. Far downstairs, a doorman beneath the awning, staring uptown.

The Air in August

Think of a fan feathering above a bed, a woman sleeping under the blades turning, how the breeze comes thin and sibilant, secrets spoken too softly to be heard, her shoulders caressed by the hand of the wind. Think of her shifting and arching her back in silence. Her damp face touched by falling layers of air, her body veiled by a welcome chill. The night outside heavy with summer. The trees wilting. A full moon or a wash of stars or a speck of cloud against the blackness. Something on the fan just barely vibrating, the chain that accounts for the strength of the breeze, the way it all works.

Anne Whitehouse

The Gulf of Mexico has been an important landscape for me since my early childhood. I was born and grew up in Alabama, and my family vacationed on the Florida panhandle. In addition, my husband's grandparents began visiting Sanibel Island many many years ago, before a bridge connected the island to the mainland. For over 30 years, I have visited Sanibel several times a year, and that beautiful island has inspired a number of my poems.

Blessing III

Some of my happiest hours
have been my pink-and-gold dawns
beachcombing for shells on Sanibel.

Looking down, I tread lightly,
trying not to crush a single shell
searching among the spoils of nature
for the delicate, defectless ones
I never tire of finding –

treasures stranded
on sands soft as flour
deliciously cold and ridged
to my bare feet.

My husband said,
"You think they are valuable,
but they are worth nothing.
I like finding them, too.
Then I put them in a closet
and never look at them."

Yet he loves them
as a family heritage,
his grandparents' beloved activity
shared with their descendants,
which he's passed on,
unexamined, like the Unconscious,
influencing his idea of himself,
knowing and naming Nature.

As for me, I never tire of looking,
I feast my eyes
and see them change
in my perception.
Collected and sorted
in the drawers of my cabinet,
a thousand miles
from the sea of their birth,
they seem more beautiful
to me than works of art,
mysteries without
the animals that made them.

Blessing XXXVI

I walked out on the beach,
and there it was, right in my path—
the rare Junonia,
most prized of Sanibel shells,
winking at me in the early morning.

Not a perfect specimen—the tip gone,
some of the square
brown markings faded,
but of a decent size,
with whorls on the lip,
delicate and heavy
as if carved from stone,
on the inner curve
a lovely sheen.

I could scarcely believe it:
a shell I'd sought for thirty years
and never found was now mine.
It seemed it had come to me
without my looking for it.

So it is, I think, with so much
that we seek:
the thing will reveal itself
only in its time.

Desecration

I placed it like a reminder
in the corner of my computer screen;
all day I kept coming back to it:
the web cam a mile underwater
recording clouds and plumes of filth
expelled like an explosive diarrhea
from the bowels of the earth,
convulsive, unstoppable,
polluting the soft, blue-green waters
and pure white sands
of the warm, salt sea,
its rich, teeming, varied life—
dolphins playing at dawn,
stealthy, sinuous sharks,
fish the colors of the rainbow,
vibrant corals and seaweeds,
mollusks and crustaceans,
the most magnificent birds
and intricate shells—
fouled and mired in the earth's shit.

The very substance of our greed
come back to contaminate the world,
until the last fires of internal combustion
are quenched.

Harold Whit Williams

Several years before I was born, my parents moved from rural north Alabama to Panama City, Florida. My father had landed a job directing the local high school marching band, and my mother, being the dutiful wife, accompanied him. Before too long, my sister came into the world.

The three of them lived for several years in the back of an old bungalow, just a few sand-strewn blocks from the bayside pier where my father fished most early mornings. To this day, he still speaks in dreamlike wonderment of the surreal creatures he pulled from the surf there—croakers, chofers, stingrays, etc. But homesickness and the lure of family ties brought my mother and father and sister back to north Alabama, to Muscle Shoals, shortly before I was born. So close! I was almost a sandy-haired beach bum Floridian.

But I'm thankful for my Muscle Shoals upbringing. That area has a rich musical heritage, and I followed suit, woodshedding the electric guitar in local garage bands and even getting a session at the R & B mecca, Fame Recording Studio. After college, I moved to Austin, Texas to further my guitar misadventures.

Austin is only a three-hour drive from the coastal bend surf. My wife and I hardly miss a year of visiting the coast, from Galveston to South Padre, but mostly Port Aransas. We stuff ourselves on the local catch, drink too much, and spy brown pelicans in their bombardier formation patrolling the blue skies.

I have been lucky enough to see the Mediterranean, Sea of Japan, and swim in the Atlantic and Pacific, but the creative pulse of my life seems set to the rhythm of the Gulf of Mexico.

Still Life with Methodist Youth Retreat and Tropical Depression

Gulf Shores, Alabama 1984

The Gulf is choppy meeting Mobile Bay.
It's stippled with our bodies, pasty white
And fattened up. We're tiger shark entrees!
We're victims of the jellyfish! We fight
As men for looks at sweet and pretty Alice.
Her body's changed; her breasts came in this summer
And seem to be more interesting than Jesus
Or anything else that preacher says. A bummer
Is the sermon after dinner. How could God
Have made so many big mistakes, I wonder —
Our science teacher's cancer in the head,
Our neighbors taken in that crash. And thunder
Is not an answer, but a question. The boy
Beside my bed lets farts and laughs for joy.

Yonder Cries the Gull

Out past the breakers
Seabirds glide and laugh,
Scoffing at civilization's creep.
At night you hear them in dunes
Murmuring threats against the state.
In the morning a peach sun
Performs chin-ups on a Texaco rig,
Flexing its solar muscles
For the sickly moon as an
Oceanographer's prop plane
Seeds clouds and drags a banner
That reads-
WIND IS BORN HERE.

Bones in the Bathwater

Knee-deep in a tepid surf,
Six a.m. on the Texas coast.
A plastic medical waste baggy
Nudges my left shin, a bobbing
Futuristic jellyfish. The Gulf
Is an oversized tub of Valvoline
Motor oil, Roundup weed killer,
Happy Meal freedom fry grease
And cremated remains of beloved pets.
Karankawa once haunted these dunes,
Mud-covered to repel mosquitoes.
Drinking holly berry tea to see God,
They believed the ocean was created
From falling tears of seagulls.
They sang many sorrowful songs
While sucking the bone marrow
Of shipwrecked Spaniards.

Contributors' Notes

Bruce Alford is a personal trainer, aerobics instructor and a former journalist, and has published creative nonfiction and poetry in various literary journals. His book of poems, *Terminal Switching* (Elk River Review Press), was published in 2007. He was an assistant professor of creative writing at the University of South Alabama for nine years where he taught a full schedule of classes, including British and American Literature, Poetry Writing and Creative Non-Fiction. He is a reviewer for *First Draft*, a publication of the Alabama Writers' Forum.

Born to a Mexican mother and Jewish father, **Rosebud Ben-Oni** is a 2013 CantoMundo Fellow. A Leopold Schepp Scholar at New York University, she won the Seth Barkas Prize for Best Short Story and The Thomas Wolfe/Phi Beta Kappa Prize for Best Poetry Collection. She was a Rackham Merit Fellow at the University of Michigan where she earned her MFA in Poetry, and was a Horace Goldsmith Scholar at the Hebrew University of Jerusalem. A graduate of the 2010 Women's Work Lab at New Perspectives Theater, her plays have been produced in New York City, Washington DC and Toronto. Her work appears or is forthcoming in *Arts & Letters, Bayou, B O D Y, Borderlands: Texas Poetry Review, Lana Turner Journal* and *Puerto del Sol*. She writes the series "On 7 Train Love" for the blog of *Sundog Lit*. Nominated twice for the Pushcart Prize, her debut book of poems, *Solecism*, was published by *Virtual Artists Collective* in March 2013. Rosebud is a co-editor for *Her Kind* at VIDA: Women in Literary Arts. Find out more about her at 7TrainLove.org.

Ash Bowen's first collection of poems, *The Even Years of Marriage*, won the 2012 Orphic Prize for Poetry and is available from Dream Horse Press. He lives in Alabama where he teaches undergraduate creative writing and literature at the University of Alabama in Tuscaloosa.

Bredt Bredthauer is a touring bicyclist and amateur competitive eater. He earned a BA from the University of Texas, an MA in English from the University of North Texas, and an MFA from the University of Florida. After quitting his job as an instructor of English, Bredthauer has spent the last year slowly bicycling around the world. He lives in a tent and has no permanent job or source of income. Since leaving his hometown of Austin last June, Bredthauer has traveled through the US, Europe, and Asia. He is currently in Istanbul debating his next destination.

Susan Cerulean awaits the birth of her new memoir, *Coming to Pass*, which addresses loss and beauty on the north Florida coastline.

Adam Clay is the author of *A Hotel Lobby at the Edge of the World* (Milkweed Editions, 2012) and *The Wash* (Parlor Press, 2006). A third book of poems, *Stranger*, is forthcoming from Milkweed Editions. His poems have appeared or are forthcoming in *Boston Review, Ploughshares, Denver Quarterly, Iowa Review, New Orleans Review,* and elsewhere. He co-edits *TYPO Magazine* and lives in Kentucky.

Brittany Nicole Connolly is currently pursuing her MFA in creative writing at the University of Tampa, while still managing to live in the hills of Greeneville, Tennessee. She is 24 years old, an avid cat devotee, and a lover of all things creative, bizarre, and fabulist. She is an *Artisan Review* editor at *Connotation Press: An Online Artifact* and her work can be found in issues of *Quarter After Eight, The Sheepshead Review, Paper Darts, The Alarmist, Scissors & Spackle,* and others.

Peter Cooley is the author of eight books of poetry, seven of them from Carnegie Mellon, and that press will bring out his ninth, *Night Bus to the Afterlife*, in 2014. He is Professor of English, Director of Creative Writing and Senior Mellon Professor in the Humanities at Tulane University.

Daniel Corrie's poems have appeared in *The American Scholar, Hudson Review, Nation, New Criterion, Shenandoah, Southern Review, Southwest Review, Virginia Quarterly Review,* among others. One of his poems received the first-place Morton Marr Poetry Prize for a formal poem. Aralia Press published a long poem of his in a chapbook edition. His essay "What Is Human Time?" appeared in *The Hudson Review,* and an essay about rhyme was reprinted in the *Able Muse Anthology*.

Meri Culp has been published in various journals, including *Quinebaug Valley Review* (forthcoming), *Espresso Ink, About Place, Cider Press Review, Southeast Review, Apalachee Review, BOMB, Painted Bride Quarterly, Rose & Thorn, Nomads, Snug, The Northeast Chronicle, Asp,* and *Sweet: A Literary Confection.* Her poems have also appeared online in *True/Slant, Poets for Living Waters,* and *USA Today* and in the anthologies *North of Wakulla* and *Think: Poems for Aretha Franklin's Inauguration Day.* She was also a runner-up in The Peter Meinke Poetry Prize competition for her collection *Cayenne Warning*.

Gwendolyn Edward is currently a MA candidate in Creative Writing at the University of North Texas where she works with *American Literary Review* and *North Texas Review*. Her speculative fiction has appeared in *Jersey Devil Press, Lissette's Tales of the Imagination, Circa, The Copperfield Review*, and others, including anthologies. She also edits the online genre publication *Deimos e-Zine*, and you can find her at gwendolynedward.com.

Ann Fisher-Wirth's fourth book of poems, *Dream Cabinet*, was published by Wings Press (2012). Her other books are *Carta Marina, Five Terraces, Blue Window*, and the chapbook *Slide Shows*. She is coeditor with Laura-Gray Street of the groundbreaking, *The Ecopoetry Anthology*, published in 2013 by Trinity University Press. Her poems have appeared widely and have received numerous awards, including the Mississippi Institute of Arts and Letters Poetry Prize, two MAC Poetry Awards, and twelve Pushcart nominations. She has had senior Fulbrights to Switzerland and Sweden, and in 2006 she was President of the Association for the Study of Literature and Environment. She teaches at the University of Mississippi, where she also directs the minor in Environmental Studies; also she teaches yoga at Southern Star in Oxford, MS.

Brett Foster is the author of two books of poetry, *The Garbage Eater* (Triquarterly Books/Northwestern University Press, 2011), and *Fall Run Road*, which was awarded Finishing Line Press's Open Chapbook Prize, and was recently released. His writing has appeared in *Boston Review, IMAGE, Iron Horse Literary Review, Kenyon Review, Pleiades, Poetry Daily, Raritan, Shenandoah, Subtropics*, and *Southwest Review*.

Rebecca Morgan Frank's first collection of poetry is *Little Murders Everywhere* (Salmon 2012), a finalist for the Kate Tufts Discovery Award. Her poems have appeared in such places as *Guernica, Ploughshares, The Georgia Review, Blackbird*, and *Best New Poets 2008*, and her new manuscript-in-progress was awarded the Poetry Society of America's Alice Fay di Castagnola Award. She teaches at the University of Southern Mississippi's Center for Writers and edits the online magazine *Memorious*.

J. Bruce Fuller is a Louisiana native. His chapbooks include *Notes to a Husband* (Imaginary Friend Press 2013), *Lancelot* (Lazy Mouse Press 2013), and *28 Blackbirds at the End of the World* (Bandersnatch Books 2010). He is the co-editor of *Vision/Verse 2009-2013: An Anthology of Poetry* (Yellow Flag Press 2013). His poems have appeared at *Crab Orchard Review, Harpur Palate, Pembroke Magazine, Yankee Pot*

Roast, The Louisiana Review, burntdistrict, The Lilliput Review, and *The Dead Mule School of Southern Literature,* among others. He has twice been nominated for Best of the Net.

Natalie Giarratano received her MFA and PhD in creative writing from Western Michigan University. Her first collection of poems, *Leaving Clean,* won the 2013 Liam Rector First Book Prize in Poetry and will be published in late spring 2013 (Briery Creek Press). Recent poems appear in *American Literary Review, Laurel Review, and Hayden's Ferry Review,* among others. D.A. Powell selected her work for inclusion in the 2011 edition of *Best New Poets,* and she is the winner of the 2011 Ann Stanford Poetry Prize from *Southern California Review.* She co-edits *Pilot Light* — an online journal of 21st century poetics and criticism, teaches writing at American University, and lives in Northern Virginia with her husband, Zach Green, and their pup, Miles.

Joshua Gottlieb-Miller holds an MFA in poetry from the University of Houston, where he was a poetry editor for *Gulf Coast: A Journal of Literature and Fine Arts.* Most recently he was a MacDowell Fellow. His work has appeared in *Indiana Review,* where he was awarded the 2012 *Indiana Review* Poetry Prize, *Blackbird, A Poetry Congeries, The Journal, Birmingham Poetry Review, Linebreak,* and elsewhere.

Jeff Grieneisen is an assistant professor of English, literature and creative writing at State College of Florida. He earned his MFA from University of New Orleans. MAMMOTH Books published his first book of poetry, *Good Sumacs,* in 2011. He is co-founder and associate editor of the annual literary journal *Florida English*, and he co-authored, with his wife Courtney, articles on Edgar Allan Poe for *Harold Bloom's Biocritiques* series (Chelsea House) and *Critical Insights: The Tales of Poe* (EBSCO/Salem). Among many journals and anthologies, his poetry has been published in Portuguese translation in the Brazilian academic journal *Revisto Espaço Acadêmico.* He has also published scholarship on the poetry of Ezra Pound. He divides his time between southwest Florida and western Pennsylvania.

Miriam Bird Greenberg is the author of *All night in the new country* (Sixteen Rivers Press, 2013). Her poems have appeared in *Poetry, Ninth Letter, Sycamore Review,* and *Zyzzyva.* She's held fellowships from the Provincetown Fine Arts Work Center, the Poetry Foundation, the National Endowment for the Arts, and was a Wallace Stegner Fellow at Stanford University. A native Texan, she teaches ESL in the San Francisco Bay Area, though she's also ridden freight trains across the United States and deckhanded aboard sailboats.

Glenn Halak started writing poetry and painting very early, inspired by his great-grandmother's poetry and paintings. He's had a book of poems published by an online publisher—writerswebpress—back in 1998 and has had poems published over the years. Three children's books, some plays produced and lately two one-acts published, some short fiction as well, are out in the world. He's had many shows of his paintings.

Carolyn Hembree's debut collection, *Skinny*, was published by Kore Press in 2012. Individual poems have appeared in *Gulf Coast, jubilat, Poetry Daily, Verse Daily,* and other journals and anthologies. Carolyn grew up in Tennessee and Alabama. Before completing her MFA, she found employment as a cashier, housecleaner, cosmetics consultant, telecommunicator, actor, receptionist, paralegal, coder, and freelance writer. She teaches at the University of New Orleans and serves as Poetry Editor of *Bayou*.

Katherine Hoerth is the author of three poetry books: *The Garden, Uprooted* (Slough Press, 2012) and two chapbooks titled *Among the Mariposas* (Mouthfeel Press, 2010) and *The Garden of Dresses* (Mouthfeel Press, 2012). Her work has been published in journals including *Boxcar, Rattle,* and *Front Porch*. She teaches writing at The University of Texas Pan American and serves as Assistant Poetry Editor of *Fifth Wednesday Journal*. She lives in deep South Texas.

Thomas Alan Holmes, a member of the East Tennessee State University English faculty, lives and writes in Johnson City, Tennessee. Some of his work has appeared in *Louisiana Literature, Valparaiso Poetry Review, The Connecticut Review, The Appalachian Journal, Seminary Ridge Review, The Florida Review, Blue Mesa Review, The Black Warrior Review, Cape Rock Journal,* and *The Southern Poetry Anthology Volume III: Contemporary Appalachia*.

Alice Johnson's stories and poems have been anthologized in *The National Story Project*, edited by Paul Auster, and *Kakalak, An Anthology of Carolina Poets*. She was an International Merit Award Winner for *The Atlanta Review's* 2012 poetry competition. She won first prize in the Tennessee Writer's Alliance for her short story "A Soft Tread." She won honorable mentions in two New Millenium Writings Contests. Poems, short stories and non-fiction have appeared in *The Great Smokies Review, The Lyricist, The Crucible, Pembroke* Magazine, *The Guilford Review, Maypop,* and the *O.Henry Festival of Stories*.

John Lambremont, Sr. is a Pushcart Prize-nominated poet from Baton Rouge, Louisiana, where he serves as editor of *Big River Poetry Review* (http://bigriverpoetry.com). John has a B.A. in Creative Writing and a J.D. from Louisiana State University, and he is the author of four full-length volumes of poetry. His work has been published internationally in many reviews and anthologies, including *The Chaffin Journal, The Mayo Review, Picayune, The Louisiana Review, Words & Images, A Hudson View,* and *Taj Mahal Review*. John has work forthcoming in *The Minetta Review, The Zip Code Project,* and *The Ampersand Review*. His blog of his previously published poems can be found at http://jlambremontpoet.blogspot.com.

Chip Livingston is the mixed-blood Creek author of two collections of poetry, *Crow-Blue, Crow-Black,* and *Museum of False Starts*. His collection of short stories, *Naming Ceremony*, is forthcoming in Spring 2014. Chip grew up on the Florida-Alabama border and now lives in Colorado, where he teaches writing online and is a faculty mentor in the low-rez MFA program at Institute of American Indian Arts.

Cleopatra Mathis' most recent collections are *White Sea* (2005) and *Book of Dog* (2013), both published by Sarabande Books. Sheep Meadow Press published her first five books of poems. Her work has appeared widely in anthologies, textbooks, magazines, and journals. Various awards include two National Endowment for the Arts fellowships, two Pushcart Prizes, and a Guggenheim Fellowship. Since 1982, she has taught creative writing and English at Dartmouth College, where she is the Frederick Sessions Beebe '35 Professor in the Art of Writing.

A seven-time Pushcart-Prize nominee and National Park Artist-in-Residence, **Karla Linn Merrifield** has had some 400 poems appear in dozens of journals and anthologies. She has ten books to her credit, the newest of which are *Lithic Scatter and Other Poems* (Mercury Heartlink) and *Attaining Canopy: Amazon Poems* (FootHills Publishing). Forthcoming from Salmon Poetry is *Athabaskan Fractal and Other Poems of the Far North*. Her *Godwit: Poems of Canada* (FootHills) received the 2009 Eiseman Award for Poetry and she recently received the Dr. Sherwin Howard Award for the best poetry published in *Weber - The Contemporary West in 2012*. She is assistant editor and poetry book reviewer for *The Centrifugal Eye* (www.centrifugaleye.com), a member of the board of directors of TallGrass Writers Guild and Just Poets (Rochester, NY), and a member of the New Mexico State Poetry Society. Visit her blog, Vagabond Poet, at http://karlalinn.blogspot.com.

A native of Mississippi, **Benjamin Morris** is the author of numerous works of poetry, fiction, and nonfiction, with recent work in such publications as the *Oxford American, the Southern Quarterly,* and the *Tulane Review*. A member of the Mississippi Artist Roster, he is the recipient of a poetry fellowship from the Mississippi Arts Commission and a residency from A Studio in the Woods in New Orleans. More information is available at http://benjaminalanmorris.com.

Heather Newberry is a graphic designer, web designer, singer, and church secretary. Her other design credits include the covers of Justin Evans' *Hobble Creek Almanac* (Aldrich Press, 2013) and Jeff Newberry's *Brackish* (Aldrich Press, 2012). She lives in South Georgia with her husband and her son.

Brent Newsom's poems have appeared in *The Southern Review, Subtropics, PANK, The Hopkins Review, Cave Wall,* and other journals and anthologies. A Louisiana native, he earned a PhD from Texas Tech University, where he held editorial posts with *32 Poems* and *Iron Horse Literary Review*. With his wife and two children, he now lives in Oklahoma, where he is Assistant Professor of English at Oklahoma Baptist University.

Alison Pelegrin is the author of three poetry collections, most recently *Hurricane Party* (2011) and *Big Muddy River of Stars* (2007), both with the University of Akron Press. She is the recipient of a creative writing fellowship from the National Endowment for the Arts, and her poems have appeared in *Poetry, Ploughshares,* and the *Southern Review*.

Deborah Paredez is the author of the poetry volume, *This Side of Skin* (Wings Press 2002), and the award-winning critical study, *Selenidad: Selena, Latinos, and the Performance of Memory*. Her poems have appeared in *Callaloo, Crab Orchard Review, Poet Lore, Poetry,* and elsewhere. She is an Associate Professor of English at the University of Texas in Austin and the co-founder of CantoMundo, a national association for Latina/o poets.

Bin Ramke grew up at the nexus of Texas, Louisiana, and the Gulf of Mexico, but teaches now at the University of Denver and the Art Institute of Chicago. His eleventh book, *Aerial,* was published last year by Omnidawn. His first book was a Yale Younger Poets selection.

Marthe Reed is the author of three books: *(em)bodied bliss* (Moria Books 2013), *Gaze* (Black Radish Books 2010) and *Tender Box, A Wunderkammer* (Lavender Ink 2007). A fourth book, *Pleth*, a collaboration with j/j hastain, is in press (Unlikely Books) and a fifth, *Nights Reading*, will be published by Lavender Ink (2014). She has also published four chapbooks as part of the Dusie Kollektiv. An essay on Claudia Rankine's *The Provenance of Beauty: A South Bronx Travelogue* appears in *American Letters and Commentary*.

jo reyes-boitel : writer, motivator/supporter, mother, daughter to oya and obatala, rabid music listener, percussionist and lover. texas transplant, by way of minnesota | florida | mexico | cuba. jo works to actively connect everyday earth activities to the heaven that surrounds.

Billy Reynolds was born and raised in Huntsville, Alabama ("The Rocket City"). His poems have been published in *Iron Horse Literary Review, Hunger Mountain, Sewanee Theological Review,* and *Third Coast,* among others. Currently, he lives in Kalamazoo, Michigan.

Katherine Riegel has published two books of poetry, *What the Mouth Was Made For* (2013) and *Castaway* (2010). Her work has appeared in journals including *Brevity, Crazyhorse,* and *The Rumpus.* She is poetry editor for *Sweet: A Literary Confection* and teaches at the University of South Florida.

Rena Rossner was born and raised on Miami Beach, Florida, and spent many summers and vacations dipping her toes in the waters of the gulf. She is a graduate of the Writing Seminars program at The Johns Hopkins University. Her poetry and short fiction has been published or is forthcoming from *Poetica Magazine, MiPoesias, Ascent Aspirations, The 22 Magazine, Fade Poetry Journal, Exterminating Angel Press, Full of Crow* and *The Prague Revue,* among others. Her cookbook *Eating the Bible* is forthcoming from Skyhorse Publishing, September 2013.

Mary Jane Ryals is Poet Laureate of the Big Bend of Florida. She grew up around Florida's Gulf beaches. She teaches writing classes in Tallahassee, and has five books published. Her new novel, *Cold Blue Moon in Paradise*, a mystery novel with the oil spill as back drop, is currently under consideration for publication.

A native of New Orleans, **Sheryl St. Germain's** work has received several awards, including two NEA Fellowships, an NEH Fellowship, the Dobie-Paisano Fellowship, the Ki Davis Award from the

Aspen Writers Foundation, and the William Faulkner Award for the personal essay. Her poetry books include *Going Home, The Mask of Medusa, Making Bread at Midnight, How Heavy the Breath of God, The Journals of Scheherazade,* and *Let it Be a Dark Roux: New and Selected Poems.* She has also published a chapbook of translations of the Cajun poet Jean Arceneaux, Je Suis Cadien. A memoir about growing up in Louisiana, *Swamp Songs: the Making of an Unruly Woman,* was published in 2003, and she co-edited, with Margaret Whitford, *Between Song and Story: Essays for the Twenty-First Century.* Her most recent book, *Navigating Disaster: Sixteen Essays of Love and a Poem of Despair,* was released in September of 2012. She directs the MFA program in Creative Writing at Chatham University.

Danielle Sellers is originally from Key West, Florida. She has an MA from The Writing Seminars at Johns Hopkins University and an MFA from the University of Mississippi where she held the Grisham Poetry Fellowship. Her poems have appeared or are forthcoming in *Subtropics, Smartish Pace, Cimarron Review, Poet Lore, Prairie Schooner, 32 Poems,* and elsewhere. Her book, *Bone Key Elegies,* was published in 2009 by Main Street Rag. Last summer, she was awarded a Walter E. Dakin Poetry fellowship to attend the Sewanee Writers' Conference. She's editor of *The Country Dog Review* and teaches at the University of Mississippi.

Martha Serpas has published two collections of poetry, *Côte Blanche* and *The Dirty Side of the Storm.* Her work has appeared in *The New Yorker, The Nation,* and *Southwest Review,* as well as in many anthologies, including *The Art of the Sonnet* and *American Religious Poems.* A graduate and former visiting faculty of Yale Divinity School, she currently teaches in the Creative Writing Program at the University of Houston. She co-produced *Veins in the Gulf,* a documentary about Louisiana's disappearing wetlands, and serves as a hospital trauma chaplain.

Paul Siegell is the author of three books of poetry: *wild life rifle fire, jambandbootleg,* and *Poemergency Room.* Paul is a senior editor at *Painted Bride Quarterly,* and has contributed to *American Poetry Review, Black Warrior Review, Coconut* and many other fine journals. Kindly find more of Paul's work – and concrete poetry t-shirts – at "ReVeLeR @eYeLeVeL" (paulsiegell.blogspot.com).

ire'ne lara silva (www.irenelarasilva.webs.com) lives in Austin, Texas, and is the author of two chapbooks: *ani'mal* and *INDíGENA.* Her first collection of poetry, *furia,* was published by Mouthfeel

Press in October 2010 and received an Honorable Mention for the 2011 International Latino Book Award in Poetry. Her first collection of short stories, *flesh to bone,* will be published by Aunt Lute Press in 2013. ire'ne is the Fiction Finalist for AROHO's 2013 Gift of Freedom Award, the 2008 recipient of the Gloria Anzaldua Milagro Award, a Macondo Workshop member, and a CantoMundo Inaugural Fellow. She and Moises S. L. Lara are currently co-coordinators for the Flor De Nopal Literary Festival.

Jay Snodgrass lives in Tallahassee with his wife and daughter. A native of Florida, he grew up in Japan. His first book is *Monster Zero,* poems about Godzilla. Just like Godzilla, Jay Snodgrass is a child of the Sea.

Andrea Spofford writes essays and poems, some of which can be found in *Paper Nautilus, The Citron Review, Blood Orange Review, Composite: Arts Magazine,* and others. Her chapbook, *Everything Combustible,* is forthcoming from Dancing Girl Press. She is assistant professor of poetry at Austin Peay State University and an editor of *Zone 3 Journal* and Press.

Sunnylyn Thibodeaux left New Orleans for San Francisco to attend, the now defunct, New College of California. She is the author of *Palm to Pine* and *As Water Sounds* (Bootstrap Press), as well as several small books including *88 Haiku for Lorca, Room Service Calls* and *Universal Fall Precautions.* She co-edits Auguste Press and Lew Gallery Editions.

Jay Udall's work has recently appeared, or is forthcoming, in *Prairie Schooner, North American Review, Verse Daily, Cincinnati Review,* and *Spillway.* His latest volume of poems, *The Welcome Table* (University of New Mexico Press), won the New Mexico Book Award. He teaches at Nicholls State University in Thibodaux, LA, where he also serves as chief editor of *Gris-Gris,* a new online journal (www.nicholls.edu/gris-gris).

Jerry Wemple is the author of two poetry collections, co-editor of the anthology *Common Wealth: Contemporary Poets on Pennsylvania,* and editor of *Watershed: the Journal of the Susquehanna.* His poetry and essays have appeared in numerous journals and anthologies. He teaches in the creative writing program at Bloomsburg University of Pennsylvania, and still dreams of patrolling the Everglades as a peace officer on an airboat.

Patti White is the author of three collections of poetry (*Tackle Box,* 2002; *Yellow Jackets,* 2007; and *Chain Link Fence,* 2013), all from Anhinga Press. Her work has also appeared in journals including *Forklift, Ohio; North American Review; River Styx; Iowa Review; Mississippi Review; New Madrid;* and *DIAGRAM*. She teaches creative writing and literary theory at the University of Alabama, where she also serves as Director of Slash Pine Press.

Anne Whitehouse (www.annewhitehouse.com) was born and raised in Birmingham, Alabama, and has been visiting the Gulf Coast since she was a child. Her husband's parents, Hugh and Martha Whitehouse, lived on Sanibel Island, a place that is close to her heart, which has found its way into her poetry, including the two Blessings from her collection, *Blessings and Curses,* included in *The Gulf Stream*. She wrote "Desecration" in response to the horrendous Deepwater Horizon oil spill of 2010. The title poem of her 2012 collection, *The Refrain,* is about her beloved Sanibel Island, and Sanibel is featured as one of the settings of her novel, *Fall Love.*

Harold Whit Williams is guitarist for the critically acclaimed rock band Cotton Mather. The 2007 book, *Shake Some Action,* rated their Kontiki album at number 26 of the Top 200 Power Pop Albums of all time, comparing the album to Revolver-era Beatles, Big Star, and Apples in Stereo. Williams' poetry chapbook, *Waiting For The Fire To Go Out,* is available from Finishing Line Press, and his poems have appeared in *Atlanta Review, Oxford American, Oklahoma Review, Carolina Quarterly, Tulane Review,* among others. He was a finalist in the *New Letters* 2012 Poetry Award and the 2013 Copperdome Chapbook Contest. He lives in Austin, Texas.

Acknowledgements

Rosebud Ben-Oni; "Returning to Sal Si Puedes" first appeared in *B O D Y*.

Peter Cooley; "From The Gulf, " "Locales," and "Meditation at Crescent Beach" from *The Room Where Summer Ends*, Carnegie Mellon University Press, 1979.

Ann Fisher-Wirth; "BP" from *Dream Cabinet*, Wings Press, 2012.

Brett Foster; "Recovery, Gulf Coast" appeared in *The City*.

Natalie Giarratano; "Low-Water Mark" from *Leaving Clean*, Briery Creek Press, 2013.

J. Bruce Fuller; "Boy, Age 9" first appeared in *burntdistrict*.

Miriam Bird Greenberg; "I Passed Three Girls Killing a Goat" first appeared in *Poetry*; "It's Hard to Forget" first appeared in the *Sycamore Review 24.2*; "Seasons Changing" first appeared in *Diagram 8.2* (as "Seasons Changing; Unanswered Questions").

Carolyn Hembree; "[O pony of South Derbigny o leaping yellow]" first appeared in *New Orleans Review*; "Fox Ode" first appeared in *Indiana Review*.

Chip Livingston; "Defuniak Springs" first appeared in *Gargoyle*; "Burn" first appeared in *Ploughshares*.

Cleopatra Mathis; "The Faithful" from *The Center for Cold Weather*, Sheep Meadow Press, 1989; "On a Shared Birthday: J.C.L. 1953-1979" from *The Center for Cold Weather*, Sheep Meadow Press, 1989; "Salt Water Ducks" from *Book of Dog*, Sarabande Books, 2013.

Karla Linn Merrifield; "1564: The Virgin One" first appeared in *The Mochila Review*.

Brent Newsom; "Smyrna" appeared in *PANK*.

Alison Pelegrin; "Pantoum of the Endless Hurricane Debris," "Hurricane Party," and "Ode to the Pelican" from *Hurricane Party*, University of Akron Press, 2011.

Deborah Paredez; "The Gulf, 1987" appeared in *Poetry*.

Marthe Reed; "lapse :: a city" first appeared in *The Offending Adam*.

Katherine Riegel; "And That Life" appeared in *Sandhill Review*.

Sheryl St. Germain; "Lake Pontchartrain" from *Making Bread at Midnight*, Slough Press, 1992; "Crossing the Atchafalaya" appeared in *Crab Orchard Review*; "Midnight Oil" appeared in *Interim*.

Danielle Sellers; "December Evening, Key West" from *Bone Key Elegies*, Main Street Rag, 2009.

Paul Siegell; "05.04.07 – New Orleans Jazz Vipers –Spotted Cat, NOLA" and "05.05.07 – Jonathan Freilich, Skerik, Stanton Moore, Todd Sickafoose & Mike Dillon – Chickie Wah Wah, NOLA" appeared as a limited-edition broadside, Splitleaves Press, 2010.

ire'ne lara silva; "tierra" from *ani'mal*, Axoquentlatoa Press, 2010.

Sunnylynn Thibodeaux; "Evangeline, How Do You Call Your Tribe" and "Not Quite Colorado Bound" first appeared in *Death and Life of American Cities*.

Patti White; "Sarasota" appeared in *Hobble Creek Review*.

Anne Whitehouse; "Blessing III" and "Blessing XXXVI" from *Blessings and Curses*, Poetic Matrix Press, 2009; "Desecration" from *The Refrain*, Dos Madres Press, 2012.

Snake~Nation~Press wishes to thank the
poets and editors who made this book possible.